JUL 20 2011

Teaching, the Hardest Job You'll Ever Love!

Helpful Ideas for Teachers In and Out of the Classroom

Steve Sonntag

ROWMAN & LITTLEFIELD EDUCATION
A division of
ROWMAN & LITTLEFIELD PUBLISHERS, INC.
Lanham • New York • Toronto • Plymouth, UK

This book was placed by the Educational Design Services LLC literary agency.

Published by Rowman & Littlefield Education
A division of Rowman & Littlefield Publishers, Inc.
A wholly owned subsidary of The Rowman & Littlefield Publishing Group, Inc.
4501 Forbes Boulevard, Suite 200, Lanham, Maryland 20706
http://www.rowmaneducation.com

Estover Road, Plymouth PL6 7PY, United Kingdom

British Library Cataloguing in Publication Information Available

Library of Congress Cataloging-in-Publication Data
Sonntag, Steve.
    Teaching, the hardest job you'll ever love : helpful ideas for teachers in and out of the classroom / Steve Sonntag.
       p. cm.
    ISBN 978-1-60709-738-9 (cloth : alk. paper) – ISBN 978-1-60709-739-6 (pbk. : alk. paper) – ISBN 978-1-60709-740-2 (electronic)
    1. Teaching–Handbooks, manuals, etc. I. Title.
    LB1025.3.S66 2010
    371.102–dc22

                                                                        2010011256

∞ ™ The paper used in this publication meets the minimum requirements of American National Standard for Information Sciences—Permanence of Paper for Printed Library Materials, ANSI/NISO Z39.48-1992.

Printed in the United States of America

Teachers are like mirrors because they reflect what the students do and what they don't do.

—Steve Sonntag

~

Contents

Acknowledgments

Teaching, the Hardest Job You Will Ever Love!: Helpful Ideas for Teachers In and Out of the Classroom is dedicated to many people whose focus and devotion are to making our schools run smoothly and efficiently.

Outside the classroom environment, administrators on the school site, at the district office, and at the county office have a major role to fulfill by managing the varied demands that they are given by society and to work with their superiors, their staffs, students, and parents and guardians. Counselors have a tremendous task to cope with their students' personal and academic lives. School psychologists deal with students' emotional struggles and assess any learning problems that students may have. Reading specialists and speech therapists patiently focus their expertise on individual students. All of these overseers accomplish a great deal of work with time and dedication.

The administrative secretarial staffs deal with all members of the educational community with grace and respect, although it can be a major challenge for them to maintain their sanity at times. They truly are amazing to efficiently help with the school's continuous changes.

Schools have been dramatically affected financially with limited resources, thus making it extremely difficult to provide quality, educated students. The school society truly has its hands full. Yet, the school society manages it all as well as they can, and they are all to be congratulated for their tremendous dedication and effort.

Schools contend with the societal pressures upon our youth: negative attitudes, behavior problems, drugs, alcohol, smoking, gangs, peer pressure, teen pregnancies, all forms of abuse, family issues, special education needs, and students from other countries oftentimes struggling to learn English, but not always.

Students usually do their best to balance a personal life along with their normal school responsibilities. There is a whole wide assortment of personalities, and they can be very mature, somewhat mature, immature, or very immature, thus making the teachers' job a major challenge. Luckily, many truly do see the advantages of learning in the high school environment. As for those who prefer to try to create problems, they will hopefully learn that the school community is for all students and wish them to have a brighter future with their assistance.

Parents deal with their offsprings to give them amazing support in all forms, and they need to be applauded for their dedication. Nevertheless, there are those parents who have the best of intentions possibly at first, but begin to lose interest in parenting and/or have major issues of their own, thus potentially creating major problems of tremendous consequences for their young adults as they mature.

Guardians related and not related to the young adults and group home managers are the other keepers of our youth who oftentimes have major struggles, and they truly deserve to be recognized and respected for their continuous guidance of troubled youth.

Campus monitors continually are amazing, because they need to make sure that students are safe, that they get to their classes on time, and that they remain in class during the school day. They do an amazing job of knowing students and to be patient and to be persistent in their duties.

Cafeteria staffs are the feeders of the entire school community oftentimes before school and during the school day. They are fantastic in the way they are able to handle their daily obligations.

Custodians work at various times of the school day, and they also clean the school grounds after school for organizations, sports, dances, and night classes. Considering that there have been cutbacks even in the custodial staff, it is truly amazing that they have been able to clean the campus as well as they have.

Related to the classroom, librarians are the "Jacks and Jills of their trade", being the resources for all kinds of information in books and in electronic media. Their jobs are very demanding based on the needs of the students as well as of the teachers. They truly are appreciated for their flexibility in helping the entire educational community.

Oftentimes, schools have computer assistants who help students and teachers in computer labs. Like librarians, computer assistants complete their jobs utilizing their expertise so that students and teachers may be able to work on projects and to browse the Internet. They too are to commended for their dedication and for their time.

PTSA organizations do the best they can to be supportive of the entire school community via activities and funding. They definitely can be helpful and understanding of what administrators and teachers are trying to accomplish in the school environment.

Inside the classroom environment, teachers share their knowledge with their students hoping for their academic success and their appropriate behavior. They amazingly become the classroom managers whose divergent ways of presenting the information can be instrumental for student success.

Some teachers are fortunate to have adult aides working with individual students or with small groups. They are to be applauded for their time and for their patience.

Coaches involved with sports and academics dedicate so many hours to their causes, and they truly can be inspirations for the youth of today.

Local, state, and national educational organizations are the fabulous umbrellas that give their dedicated support to the educational community with the assistance of journals, e-mails, and conferences. They are to be commended for having resources available.

I would also like to dedicate this book to specific people who have been very influential in the field of education and personally significant for me throughout the years, and I am forever grateful for each of them.

In my formative years, I honor my junior high counselor Mr. Osegueda, and my Spanish teachers Mr. Harvey, Mrs. Cannon, and Mr. La Torre.

In the most recent years, I honor our educational community including Pam Clemensen, our former administrators including Vahl Clemensen, our former principal Bill Jones, our current high school principal Doug Mc-Creath, our former Career Career counselor Joe Mora, Linda Adair, John Alameda, Andy Anderson, Rick Arucan, the Barker family, Bob Bechill, Lynn Beck, Paul and Bonnie Bennett, Louis Bohn, Bonnie Bryson, Chuck Benson, John Bradbury, the Brophy family, Marie Buccolo, Tim Buchanan, the Cadle family, Ann Carr, Marcia Chapman, Barbara Chiapale, Laurie Coates, Ruth Crawford, Dale Cretser, the Crumb family, Lita Custodio, Carol De Sa Campos, Meredith Davis, the DeGroot family, Gary Dei Rossi, Butch and Martha Dias-Linn, Samuel and Mindie Dolson, Scott Eckerle, Dick Edwards, Will Eggerer, Sandy Elder, Denise Elling, Vicki Evans, Arte Fairbanks, Stuart Farrell, and the Fejer family.

The honors' list continues with Ed Fichtner, Terry Fix, Dan and Mickie Flores, Mick Founts, Sarah Fox, Jeff Gaines, John Gibson, Kirt Giovannoni,

Suzanne Glick, Terry Godinez, Rachel Gomez, Jolene Giovannoni, Sandy Greenblatt, Barbara Guardado, Sharon Giudice, Michelle Halla, Joe Handy, Julianne Harper, Leslie Harris, Tish Hart, Diane Haynes, Mike and Barbara Henry, Tia Hermosillo, Tom Hopkins, Doug Horton, Angela Hotchkiss, Jim Hughes, Jared Hunt, Ron Hurick, Ron Inderbitzin, Katy Jesus, Paul and Louise Kantro, Art Johnson, Joe Johnson, Kathy Johnson, Teresa Johnson, Trulen Karnes, Vanessa Knepp, Butch Linn, Carl Lutz, Santiago Macario, Blanca Malaspina, Lili Maldonado, Melanie Marino, Armen and Vickie Markarian, Jill Martin, Pat Mayorga, Dolores McCabe, Mike McCullough, Mary Mello, Cinder Merritt, Jack Miller, and Stan and Lynee Monckton.

The honors also go to Robyn Moore, Dorothy Mulvihill, Lisa Miscione, Harry Nagy, Nina Norton, Fernando Nunez, Christine O-Rourke, Sam Ousley, Michelle Padilla, Sharen Petrig, Earl Pimentel, Annemarie Platt, the Poulos family, the Ragan family, Eric Reis, Greg Risso, George Rose, and Diane Rothchild, Brenda Rushing, Mary Salisbury, Warren Sapir, Daylin Seals, Tony and Yolanda Serna, Irv Shaw, Ann Snell, Patricia Stewart, Adele Stinson, Jim Stoker, the Stonehockers, Bo Svoboda, Curt Swenson, Donna Taylor, Rose Thomas, Warren and Effie Toney, Clairlyse Touchon, Laurie Toy, Ann Tuliao, the Vavra family, Dru Vignolo, Ai Vu, Kristy Wagner, Rick Wentworth, Helen Yost, Madalyn Youngbird, Steve Winter, and Darleen Zimmerman.

The rest of staffs of both Manteca High School and Presentation School, the PTSA organization, all of the rest of my former students, and all of the parents and guardians of both schools truly deserve to be recognized for their work and for their dedication.

Dr. Edward Brasmer was our amazingly sincere, devoted principal for twenty-two years at Manteca High School in Manteca, California. His focus was personal worth and high, realistic expectations as his goals in his life on behalf of our school, and he truly was our role model.

In my personal life, I especially wish to honor and show recognition to my parents Lewis and Natalie Sonntag, Hans Sontag, my first family including my first wife Pearl Sonntag, Marissa Peterson and Sabrina Sonntag Canadell, Julius and Ethel Adler, Marge Adler, Paul Adler, Sue Adler, Gail Buffington, Marvin and Dorothy Cohen, David and Randi Jaspan, Louis and Florence Krieger, Michelle Owen, Hyman and Zelda Plotkin, Ulla Rychter, Art and Juliet Yaspan, Bert and Renee Yaspan, Bob Yaspan, Gerson and Rita Yaspan, Lorraine Yaspan, Peter Yaspan, all of their families, and our dearly beloved grandmother Rebecca Yaspan.

My personal honors' list concludes with my second family, including my second wife Ruby Sonntag, to her daughters Brenna and Brittany Joe,

Dorothy Lew, Herman Lew, Judy Lew, Linda Lew and their families, to our close friends Tu Bears, Woody Brown, Mike Forman, Richard Harty, Arlene Krauss, Leo and Aziza Mara, the Shalom-Nautico community including Pat Andrews, Bev Breakey, Jerry Hackett, Charley and Sally Lindberg, Steve Sheppard, the Thursday men's group, and Dee Ann Traum.

I owe my deepest gratitude to all of the previously mentioned, and I have the utmost respect for all of them. All of them have been very helpful throughout my life. They truly have been my role models. They certainly have been role models for the people whom they have served throughout the years.

~

CHAPTER ONE

The Purpose of *Teaching, the Hardest Job You'll Ever Love!*

Having role models in life is an essential source for our society. They can be people who can contribute in everlasting positive or negative ways. Positive role models earn their respect by showing how to be decent, caring, trustworthy, sincere, and reliable individuals by what they say and by what they do for the sake of the people whom they encounter. There are unfortunately negative role models; they are only interested in themselves and will try to take advantage of others or try to hurt them in some way.

Being a positive role model as a teacher can be based on many factors. One's parents or guardians can give love, support, encouragement, praise, attention, care, respect, patience, and time. One's former teachers could have been so dynamic in their teaching methodology and/or by the extra care and attention that they genuinely displayed to their students. Friends can also be very influential for prospective teachers.

A previous teacher could have actually inspired a student to become a teacher due to something very derogatory that was stated. This negative remark could have sparked someone to not follow that example and to be forever cognizant of the importance of encouragement and praise. There might have been such abhorrent behavior by a teacher toward students that a current teacher chooses to truly make a positive difference in the lives of young people.

Whoever or whatever was the deciding factor for wanting to teach, you are to be congratulated for your desire to become a teacher. You have decided to become a role model to students so that they can learn that much more about your subject area with the additional learning tools of self-respect, self-accountability, respect for others, and interdependence.

Teachers are overburdened with the major demands they endure daily. They have a limited budget, which oftentimes requires them to purchase materials on their own, if they so desire. They oftentimes must take classes in order to meet state and national standards and also for salary advancement. Many need to align their curriculum with fellow teachers daily according to specific state and national standards, even though there may be students who simply will fail to understand the material very well and simply need more time and more practice. They have large classes. They attend a multitude of meetings above and beyond teaching in the classroom environment.

Teachers learn how to motivate students to become inspired by the curriculum, while being keenly aware of the need to be respectful, tactful, and patient. Students learn at different rates, oftentimes requiring different modalities of learning, all of which can be a major challenge.

Teachers are heavily inundated with frequent testing, thereby requiring them to teach to the test. If they succeed by having their students achieve the required levels of proficiency, great; however, if they fail to achieve them, there are more demands imposed on them to try to improve on the next test. When these goals are not met, there can be changes in the status of the school's worthiness; changes in terms of the administrators, the teachers, the students being transferred to other schools; and public scrutiny by the media. What the general public fails to realize is that the student population can make or break a school's reputation.

Teaching, The Hardest Job You Will Ever Love! can help you as a teacher by giving suggestions as to how to maintain your enthusiasm while still enjoying your personal life. This book offers realistic ways to make positive changes to help teachers and students alike. Teaching is a continuous process of reaching and inspiring students. Learning is an endless process for your students as well as for yourself. Caring can be provided by the entire dedicated school community in order to give students personal attention, along with emphasizing the importance of responsibility and interdependence. In turn, the school's student population can have more successes.

This book's name, *Teaching, The Hardest Job You Will Ever Love!*, is important to reflect upon. While teaching can be very demanding, you can love the challenge of reaching out to students in order to extend their horizons in terms of their self-worth and in terms of their knowledge of the outside world. A majority of the time, teachers will encounter various degrees of success in educating students, while there can be students who cannot learn or refuse to learn, based on their study habits, based on their attitude about themselves or about life in general. Beyond the academic challenge, there is the matter of discipline, which can obstruct the teachers' goal daily. They can handle discipline with ease at times and sometimes will lose hope based on the kind of students they are teaching. Thus, teaching can truly sway from pure enjoyment to extremely difficult work and pure frustration.

Here is one way to look at the challenge of being a teacher. Imagine a teacher being the captain at the front of a racing boat. He or she has already taught the students how to row and the importance of them rowing in unison in the same direction. Yet, when students still cannot seem to understand the concept of rowing or refuse to row in unison in the same direction, the captain can only encourage or warn all participants to cooperate or else they will not move. Thus, while teachers are 50 percent of the equation of the classroom environment, students are the other 50 percent of the equation. They are heavily influenced by their parents or guardians (who raise their young adults in the best way they can usually), and they can influence their young adults' attitudes about themselves and about others.

Teachers probably can be challenged by both enthusiastic and nonenthusiastic students in their classes. Enthusiastic students can be a challenge due to the fact that they are like sponges who are very inquisitive and can be rather impatient at times, or they can be very appreciative, understanding, and patient to learn the information in due time. There can be many more nonenthusiastic students who know they are required to attend school, and they prefer to be at home or hanging out with their friends, but certainly not at school.

There are different forms of media that have been quite influential on our youth. Current technological advances have produced students who enjoy e-mailing, search engines, and websites, which can influence them either positively or negatively. They also have cell phones to divert their attention from their education. Television and movies are quite influential by what is produced in terms of violence, language, and sex. Teen magazines can contribute to student attitudes, with them placing a lot of emphasis on such matters as the latest fashions and body fitness.

Peer conformity is always going to be a challenge for students who do not want to be considered outcasts and want to fit in as well as they can. In fact, they will act in ways and say things that they do not necessarily believe are correct due to their desire to be part of a group.

Student clothing and makeup trends certainly can be eye-catching, alarming, and disturbing, thus making it difficult for the entire school community to focus its attention on the goal of education. If the clothing and makeup trends are violations of the school's rules, of course, there are certain repercussions that will follow.

Students may be involved in sports with practices that can drain their ability to focus well on their studies. Luckily, there are many coaches who emphasize academics and allow time for these student-athletes to complete their assignments prior to practicing their sports.

Students may be working before or after school, which can dramatically affect their ability to learn and to get enough sleep.

Thus, you have acquired a major challenge to try to persuade your media generation students and those students who are interested in sports, work, peer pressure, and current trends to become and to remain inspired by your subject matter. To become their role model requires a lot of inner strength, assertiveness, the ability to inspire, patience, tact, and the ability to have high expectations. Also, it is highly important that mutual respect is earned and maintained to achieve academic success by students.

Each chapter of *Teaching, the Hardest Job You Will Ever Love!* is designed for a student teacher, a new teacher, a teacher of a few years' experience, or a veteran teacher of many years of experience. Like a cookbook, this book is a sampler of ideas. Please consider practicing and sampling those ideas for your own teaching style. Please feel free to modify them. It is best to remember that any changes incorporated can take time, planning, and patience.

This book is not designed as a panacea, but as a possible, positive, and realistic guide as well as a stepping stone in the right direction of making a better difference with students. All of these ideas that are presented have been tried and have been proven to be successful with a majority of students of different abilities and with a majority of students with "a chip on their shoulder." It can ultimately help them with any self-esteem issues they may have so that not only will their lives be filled with information, but they will also be motivated to become role models for others whom they will encounter in the future both personally and professionally.

CHAPTER TWO

~

Striving for a
Healthy Life as a Person

A teacher's life is so completely filled with work, and there are those teachers who thrive on this challenge. Even those energetic teachers can become burned out either slowly or quickly. It is almost like being a juggler trying to look at the knives that have been thrown up into the air and trying not to hurt oneself at the same time.

Whether a person is single, in a committed relationship, or in a committed relationship with children, squeezing some precious time to enjoy the world around oneself can be difficult, if not impossible, due to professional responsibilities.

No matter what your personal status may be, it is essential to be kind to yourself. It is exceptionally important that you, family, and friends work as a team to have a more meaningful, more enriched life. If not, physiological and psychological consequences can be the result. There can be medical problems, such as high blood pressure and diabetes. Emotional stress may be the result. Relationships may be abandoned, if too much emphasis is placed on professional duties.

We all have the biological needs to eat, to drink, and to sleep. Those are the givens of our lives. Being single, when so much time and effort are devoted to teaching, it can become very difficult to prepare a healthy meal. There can be a tendency to want to eat at a fast food restaurant on a frequent basis to get some food while maybe completing schoolwork. The only drawback with these eating lifestyles is that there can be weight gain very quickly due to such ingredients as salt and sugar, and once that happens, there will be unwanted weight and also medical problems.

A good example of the consequences of bad eating habits is the movie *Super Size Me*, showing the dramatic weight gain and eventual problems related to eating strictly fast food. If you have not seen this movie as of yet, it is well worth your while.

Several comments about sugar intake are necessary. Eating a piece of pie or a piece of cake once in a while can be very tempting, and, perhaps it is desirable for special ocassions, such as birthdays, weddings, and anniversaries. Drinking a soda or some alcohol once in a great while could be considered fine. Please do remember, however, that moderation is the key element here. The less sugar that remains in the body, the better the individual will feel and the healthier the individual will be. If you are in a committed relationship with or without children, your life is filled with that many more responsibilities along with the fulfillment of having meaningful relationships. Again, with professional lives being essential to provide food, clothing, and shelter, there may be a reliance on fast food including salt and sugar, which can lead to medical issues. Nevertheless, there is usually at least one adult in such relationships that wishes to provide healthy food.

In the event you wish to reduce your weight, it is a good idea to possibly include a friend or relative as a support system. It will become easier to support and to encourage one another. The motivation, however, has to come from within each individual.

A good way to feel full and less hungry is to hydrate oneself. Of course, drinking water constantly is not desirable while teaching due to the inevitable "nature calls." So it is important to determine the amount of water you can drink. It truly is a great way to cleanse one's system.

Fruits are very delicious and nutritious. While fruits are healthy, it is important not to indulge too much, since they do include natural sugar, which can translate into fat.

Vegetables are great for salads and just for snacking. They can be very filling, based on which kinds you like to eat.

Organic foods of all kinds can be found in many mainstream stores nowadays. While organic food can normally be more expensive than "regular" food, the benefits of organic food can keep a person healthier with a more vibrant lifestyle.

Stir fries are always good and filling. Granted, it does take a little time and effort to prepare, but if these ingredients of sliced potatoes, baby carrots, and small pieces of meat are placed into a big pot to heat up, several meals are available.

It is also essential to get enough sleep, which will result in feeling more rested and feeling more energetic. One's mood and work can be that much more positive; however, with limited amounts of sleep, the chances are very strong that a person will feel lethargic, and the mood and work can be affected negatively. Thus, please allow enough sleep on a daily basis for yourself.

By practicing good, healthy habits, you can feel that much more enthusiastic about life and become a positive role model for family, friends, and maybe even your students.

CHAPTER THREE

~

How about Moving Your Body?

Another exceptionally important ingredient is regular physical exercise. It is important to commit to exercising regularly. If you are already, that is very commendable. If not, please consider the following suggestions.

While at school, please consider working out in the gym with or without some students with the permission of the teacher during your preparation period. Or how about an energetic walk around the school grounds during preparation periods and/or part of the lunch periods with another teacher?

Exercising on a treadmill or some other form of exercise equipment at home can be beneficial.

It is advisable to buy a variety of exercise DVDs in order to not become bored with any one particular DVD.

If there is an exercise program on television on a daily basis that you enjoy and can be helpful, how about making it a point to view it either when it is actually on or to record it in order to play it later on during the day or the next morning prior to getting ready for school?

If you are more of an outdoors type of person, how about an energetic walk in a park right after school? In this way, you can relieve stress and have a more relaxed mind prior to completing any schoolwork that needs to be addressed.

Kickboxing is a very aggressive exercise to help release physical and emotional tension very quickly, and it will help you sweat a lot as well.

Aquarobic exercises at neighborhood pools or at gyms are healthy exercises because water can provide a lot of resistance to build strength.

If you enjoy dancing, please consider taking a dance class at an adult school, at a community center, or at a local college or university. It is a great way to meet new people, to enjoy dancing partners, to learn different dance steps (which also exercises the brain and body to become more coordinated), to enjoy the music played, and to get some physical exercise all at the same time.

Another form of dancing that is very unique, can be inspirational, and can help to get some exercise at the same time is called NIA, Neuromuscular Integrative Action. There are not necessarily partners at first, but there is a lot of moving around. NIA is designed to have people get in touch with inner feelings. If you are interested in NIA, please go to www.nianow.com for more details and locations. It is quite an enlightening experience, to say the least.

If you have access to a bicycle, rollerblades, skates, or a trampoline, how about utilizing them for different forms of exercises and to enjoy different parts of your neighborhood?

You may even want to combine any of these activities for variety's sake. After all, a variety of physical activities will help you not to become bored and to enjoy each one. If you have a family, please involve all of them as much as possible. It will be helpful for them by keeping them healthy and thereby solidifying your relationships.

CHAPTER FOUR

~

Mental and Emotional Workouts

Please consider any of the following mental and emotional workout possibilities that are forms of destressing.

To see if you would be interested in any of the following mental exercises, please attend an introductory class at a studio or at a gym or rent a DVD related to these methods.

Yoga can be a very invigorating experience that not only helps you mentally, but physically. If and when one sees pictures of people sitting on a floor with their eyes shut and with their hands in the prayer position, that is only a very small segment of yoga. It is a very powerful, very rigorous way to do many exercises in different positions in order to have more control of one's body movements. In turn, the mind can become more in control of the body and subsequently the emotions in certain positions, which are more challenging than one might suspect.

Pilates is another activity very worthy of consideration. Pilates exercises teach awareness of breath and alignment of your entire body. Pilates exercises can consist of mat work and working with machines that are controlled by body movements. Different movements with styrofoam cylinders, rubber balls, and weights can also be performed at home. Overall, you can acquire more strength in your body, and you can alleviate a lot of aches.

Myofascial release therapy is a very unusual form of therapy. It primarily focuses on any tension that is felt in the body, normally created by some sort of stress, whether it happened in the past, whether it is happening now, or whether it may occur in the future. Myofascial release therapy can be done with one or two trained professionals who can deal with where there is any pain or discomfort, and people may also wish to express whatever they are feeling or thinking during these sessions.

Since there is truly a connection between how the mind perceives or feels about things with the body, there can be consequential tightness that the body acquires and oftentimes absorbs for extended periods of time. In turn, myofascial release therapy can help to release a lot of physical, mental, and emotional tension that has been stored or, at least, can help you to cope with this tension easier. To find out more information about myofascial release therapy and to find a nearby therapist, please go to www.myofascialreleasetherapy.com.

Another method to have a better focus is to practice meditation. It is a great way to become better rested while still being alert and being able to react more calmly to stressful situations in life. It would be essential to learn from an instructor some of the essential techniques to make it a more effective tool. In turn, people can practice meditation individually any time during the day, even during breaks when they are alone.

Big Brothers Big Sisters is an organization that you might want to consider in order to feel that much more youthful, that much more inspired, and to become that much more a part of a young person's life. After signing up and passing their screening process, you can become a mentor to a young adult by meeting with him or her on a regular basis. It is advisable to be a mentor to a young adult who does not and will not attend your high school because you would not want to have him or her as a student. The Big Brother Big Sister relationship is different than that of a teacher and a student.

The benefits of participating in Big Brothers Big Sisters is that you and he or she can relate to one another over a relatively consistent period of time, thus helping that individual cope with life as a teenager while being able to be that much more respectful of authority figures. You can become an exceedingly important person in his or her life not only now, but also in the future. Your guidance truly can make a difference. In turn, a relationship like this can help you out that much more to understand how our youth think and feel about school and life.

Another way to be involved with youth and to exercise is to belong to a boys and girls club in your community. That could be a great way to have fun and to find out how young adults think.

As for mental challenges and inspiration, please focus on books and watching movies and television programs that are of interest to you personally and/or professionally during your free time, if you are not doing so already. They can be a lot of fun along with being very helpful in your personal life as well in your school obligations.

Of course, it is important to be selective as to what kinds of activities to consider. Please try to do your best to be consistent, if you choose to participate in any of these suggested activities.

CHAPTER FIVE

~

Relaxation Times

In this day and age, having the time to relax can become a rarity and a low priority for a teacher. You can feel truly relieved to have completed all of your professional obligations, but what about your personal obligations for relaxation?

Please consider having quality time in which a specific time period is devoted for yourself, for family, and for friends. When this is done on a regular basis, you will make this a habit. Along with the suggestions already stated in the previous chapters, please consider the following.

The idea of vacation sparks ideas of jet trips, cruises, and hiking during specific times of the year. Vacations allow people to relax and to enjoy "the fruits of their labor." Vacation time can be a time to work on projects at home. Vacation time can also be a time to reconnect with friends and family who may have been unintentionally ignored.

As for predetermined summer vacations by the school district, there are a lot of teachers who attend workshops, prepare for the next school year, and mentally prepare themselves for the onslaught of new students. Before you know it, there will remain very little time to have a great vacation away from it all.

Please consider devoting at least half of any vacation to you, your interests, your family, and your friends. Life consists of precious moments for you and for the others that are in your life, and vacation times are also for your sanity. The reason for even mentioning this is because people who are incessantly working can have difficulties learning to relax. As the vacation progresses, please consider balancing chores or jobs with actual time to relax by enjoying activities, family, and friends. After all, all work and no play is just as bad as all play and no work.

Before school begins, please try not to think of school-related activities. If you have found something that can ease your mind, please enjoy it to your heart's content. That could be doing some sort of exercise or just watching some movies and television. After all, when the new school year begins, time can pass by very quickly, and time to allow yourself to do those personal activities can be infrequent.

When it comes to other predetermined vacation times such as the winter break and the spring break, please consider completing any necessary correcting of assignments and lesson plans for the week after vacation at the earliest possible time. Then you will be able to fully relax without having to focus your thoughts on school whatsoever, and that can be a major stress reliever.

There are those teachers who believe that they simply need to delay preparing for the next school week after vacation for several days. The rationale is that they then will be able to feel more refreshed and will have a good perspective as to what they intend to accomplish for the next school week.

There are teachers who prefer to wait until the last day or the last night before school resumes. Nevertheless, if this delay causes stress and/or inefficient lesson planning, it is advisable to reconsider when to prepare for classes.

In order to preserve relaxation times for a weekend, it does require some planning. Wouldn't it be nice to have a weekend completely void of any schoolwork? To do that, it is best to organize lesson plans so that there is no work that is collected the last day of the school week. Secondly, if at all possible, you could correct work prior to the last day of the school week. Thirdly, if at all possible, you could prepare lesson plans for the following week. In turn, school and schoolwork can be left at school for the weekend, and what a relief that would be! Then you could plan whatever you personally wish or do as little as possible.

Why not also consider having vacations every day? Granted, you teach. Please consider "five-minute vacations" by thinking about a tranquil place, by thinking about a previous vacation or a desired vacation, or any other soothing thought.

This vacation activity could be just prior to getting out of bed or getting settled to go to sleep. You could have these vacationing thoughts during a moment in school when there is no one in the area. Of course, please do not drive and have your "five-minute vacations" since the focus needs to be on your driving. The "five-minute vacations" idea is similar to meditation.

Acupuncture can alleviate aches and pains and can also help with medical conditions. While there can be some justifiable apprehension about this procedure, it truly can be beneficial in the long run. For more of an explanation, it would be a good idea to get a detailed description of acupuncture from the Internet.

Another extremely important contribution to your relaxation times is if you belong to clubs that you enjoy. Not only do they fulfill your personal joy, but they are a form of escape and are a way to reenergize yourself.

The last consideration for relaxation can be your involvement in your religion by attending your place of worship and any related activities because you can relax your mind and replenish positive thoughts and goals.

So please consider the above ideas carefully for your own sake and for the sake of others around you.

~

CHAPTER SIX

The Adversarial Administration?

Managing a household can have many challenges, having to earn enough money to pay bills, to clean a household, to have and to enjoy different conveniences like a television, a cell phone, and the Internet. Managing any type of system and managing people can consist of many responsibilities. Managers have to abide by certain rules from their superiors in order to attain success as much as possible.

When the company runs smoothly, managers and their superiors are satisfied. When and if there are struggles with issues and with people, managers do the best they can to correct the errant situations, leading hopefully to better situations or people having to be reprimanded, suspended, or possibly even being fired.

A side note: the label of "administrator" should be changed. The term should be "facilitator," a person who helps another to make the job easier. In this way, everyone is helping everyone else to the best of their ability without the need of anyone being labeled superior over another. Thus, the term "school facilitator" would be representative of a support person or a guide on the side for the best interest of the school.

Even prior to possible employment, a potential teacher can feel somewhat or majorly apprehensive about school administrators. Research work is advisable and can be done by a potential teacher in order to determine which teaching positions are available. The appropriate applications are filled out to the best of one's ability in order to hopefully give a lasting, positive impression.

Upon completion, one waits for phone calls, e-mails, or letters to determine whether or not they may even wish to arrange an interview.

If the applicants are not granted an interview, then that certainly can be a letdown. There may be a number of factors for their decision. It just may very well be that they have already decided on a particular individual, and they are just publicizing these positions, which they legally are required to do. Under these circumstances, it is best to look at it from this perspective: There is even a better job possible, and it will just take a bit longer time to be considered for the interview process and eventual employment as a teacher.

If applicants are notified for an interview, it is best to give a great, lasting impression. This can be done by learning more about the community and the students in the district along with the expectations of the school and the school district.

For the actual interview, applicants should wear the best professional-looking clothes possible with nicely shined shoes. The administrators have already read the applications. They wish to validate what they have read with the interview process and to find out what kind of personality the applicants have in order to find out how they might relate to students.

During the interview, although these administrators can try to make applicants feel comfortable as much as possible, they are constantly evaluating the individuals in order to find out if they are the right ones for their school. It is best to take a nice, big, deep breath before the interview process begins in order to relax. Once it begins, answering their questions with honesty is essential because they want to be acquainted with the applicants' expectations about teaching.

Yet, if after careful consideration by the administrators, the applicants are not to be employed in their school district, it was not meant to be, and there will eventually be an even better teaching position available in the future. It is not a personal affront whatsoever.

Hopefully, they will be hired, and congratulations will definitely be in order! Administrators will then expect their contract to be read and to be signed. Also, there will be an on-site high school teacher manual that needs to be read. While the contract and manual are realistic, they also can be very demanding and overwhelming at first. They will expect rules to be adhered to. It may feel like a lot of pressure, even though the new teachers have not entered the assigned classrooms or encountered any students as of yet.

It is important to understand the school environment from the administrative perspective. The school-site administrators (principals, vice principals or assistant principals, and deans) have to deal with many different demands. They have to abide by the district, county, state, and federal goals of education just as much as teachers do. They are accountable to their own superiors at the district office just as much as teachers are. They do their best to formulate realistic rules for the teachers and the students. The administrators also have to deal with belligerent parents or guardians, students, and teachers.

Administrators have regular demands placed on them by the school's activities in which they have to arrive at school early and oftentimes remain until very late in the evening, just like teachers. Indeed, their jobs and teachers' jobs are demanding, but administrators are there to not only carry out the rules, but also to serve the entire school community along with the general public as well as possible.

Administrators have to deal with the media at various times based on the situations involved, but teachers usually do not need to deal with the media so much, unless they have special, noteworthy projects taking place or they have been directly or indirectly affected by a particular problem pertinent to the teaching environment.

When teachers have an administrator who sees his or her role as a helper with the whole school process, that kind of administrator's sole desire is to assist teachers with their goals of educating students. This is usually the type of person who is very friendly and will genuinely ask how your day has been going, for example. When it comes to this type of administrator needing teachers' assistance, he or she will usually make these requests in a respectful, tactful way. He or she is recognized and respected for being the administrator, but teachers can feel that he or she is a partner for the sake of the school community.

Many teachers have had administrators whose sole purpose is to be so irritating while still adhering to specific administrative guidelines. Oftentimes, the reason that they come across as being so stern or having a grudge is due to the fact that they wish to impress upon people that they strictly enforce the rules without wavering one iota and/or they wish to advance in administrative status. When their reputation is well known as being the strict enforcer, the district administration will regard them worthy to tackle virtually any problem and worthy of advancement of status and salary.

It is possible that they conduct themselves this way because they have been given demanding instructions to enforce the rules. It is possible that they have a vindictive personality and thus are only able to identify the so-called weaknesses in their teachers and to accentuate the negative by demoralizing them.

Under these circumstances, the best possible way to handle such negative administrators is to cooperate in the best way possible. Teachers may not like having to deal with administrators like this, but as long as teachers fulfill their professional obligations in the best way possible, it will be an easier relationship with them. Of course, if they are acting in a totally dictatorial manner, teachers do have union representatives to obtain insight and support.

In order to fulfill the obligations of attending all administrative meetings and any other school-related meetings and events, it is important to mark them in different areas as reminders. It could be important to jot down these dates and times in the lesson plan book or on different calendars, like on home calendars, school calendars, or cell phones' calendars and/or any other technological device that can give reminders. Whatever way that helps is fine so long as these meetings are attended.

One exceptionally important way that the teacher can show adherence to the rules is to be early for all meetings that the administrators schedule. It shows the administrators that the teacher is eagerly willing to listen to what is going to be expressed. At such meetings, when the time is right and when the teacher wishes to voice an opinion or a question, it too will show that the teacher is an active participant. At meetings particularly after school, it is extremely important not to doze off. It might be a good idea to have a teacher nudge another teacher in case one of them starts to doze off.

There are schools in which teachers are required to attend events, such as games, dances, and graduations, for example. Also, there usually will be forms to be filled out requested by the administration. Please be sure to fill them out very well. Should teachers have any questions, it is best to ask for clarification and to promptly turn them in by the requested dates and times.

Since there are fewer administrators and many more teachers, it is extremely important to realize that teachers are the eyes of the administration. When and if teachers see that problems do take place, like fights between students, it is important to notify the administration and campus monitors as quickly as possible. Since we live in the age of gangs and individuals who enter the campus with the purpose of creating problems of one form or another, teachers always need to be on the alert. It does not mean to seek out only the bad because there will be mostly normal days in which there may be minor problems, which teachers can easily handle.

Here is an example. When teachers notice a couple embracing and kissing one another, teachers could continue walking and say the following: "You can help each other breathe later on." While the couple would either laugh or feel a little bit embarrassed, they would unlock themselves more than likely, and teachers probably would not have that issue with them again.

This method of disciplining is much less threatening than to aggressively confront the couple by telling them in emphatic, stern ways.

When and if there is a major disturbance like a fight outside the classroom environment, observing students will wish to see who is fighting and to seemingly enjoy the fight. Under these circumstances, it is important to notify the administrators immediately and to call upon other teachers to help you disperse the observing students. With prompt notification of the administration, they and campus monitors will be able to take control of the situation in order to reduce the possibilities of injuries. It is exceedingly important not to interfere with the fighting students because no one else needs to be injured.

When there are other major disruptions such as people fleeing an area where a crime has been committed, it is again in your best interest not to interfere, but to notify the administration of the situation so that they may handle the situation and/or call the police.

When and if there are issues in your classroom in terms of student discipline, it is best to try to deal with the problems as well as you can without always referring students to the administration. Most situations can be handled by realizing what the issues are and rectifying them with a calm demeanor. Of course, if the situation is out of control, direct and quick notification of the administration is best.

The reason for bringing this to your attention is that should the administration constantly receive referrals regarding relatively minor problems from teachers, this would suggest to administrators that the teachers do not know how to appropriately manage classroom problems. That could be regarded as a so-called weakness, which would not look good on the end-of-the-year evaluations. In a future chapter, discipline will be discussed in further detail.

When and if there might be a better way to handle a certain school rule or when and if there might be an idea to share with an administrator, always share it in a tactful and respectful way and indicate the logic and the consequences of the idea.

If the idea would be considered worthy of attention, it would show the administrator that teachers have put enough thought into an idea that may work for all concerned. Even if the idea would be considered not worthy of attention, it would show that they care enough about the school's procedures, even though it may not be beneficial.

Whatever the final decision may be, this action could also serve as a way to gain that much more respect by the administration.

There is another group of administrators who teachers, generally speaking, feel more comfortable with, and they are the counselors. The counselors work with students in terms of their issues dealing with their studies, their career goals, and, oftentimes, personal issues that they have inside and outside the school environment. The counselor's job is an extremely important and extremely demanding job. They work with their superiors, the teachers, the parents, and the guardians much of the time, and they have many other responsibilities. They can really be advocates for you and for everyone else.

The administrators manage or regulate to the best of their ability with some being assistants and some being adversaries. No matter what kind of administrative staff teachers work with, teachers will be successful when they adhere to school policies to the best of their ability and focus on the academic success of their students.

CHAPTER SEVEN

~

Different Evaluation Processes

One of the many duties that principals, vice principals, assistant principals, and deans concern themselves with is the evaluation of a specified amount of staff members. First- and second-year teachers will normally have evaluations for both years while tenured teachers will typically have evaluations every other year. Of course, the process of evaluation can vary from state to state.

The usual teacher evaluation process is in the following manner. The administrator-in-charge can begin with a preobservation meeting with the teacher where objectives are discussed for the year and also when the best mutually agreeable time would be for an announced observation. Then, there is the actual observation for most of or all of the class session with a post-observation meeting, which usually deals with how the observed teacher would analyze the class session and if he or she successfully achieved the goals of that particular day and also how the administrator-in-charge assessed that class session.

There also may be one or several unannounced observations in which the administrator-in-charge may unexpectedly appear in the classroom for a full class period or less to view what is happening. Even when they do enter unexpectedly, it is always best to continue with your lesson plan so that your students' education is the focus. Of course, you will feel off-guard for a moment, but please try your best to regain your composure or your focus. The administrator is there to observe and to validate what you are doing. Typically, there will be a postobservation meeting also to assess what happened during each of these class sessions.

Please consider the following when it comes to the evaluation process. The reason that teachers are in the classroom is to teach in the best possible way on a daily basis, considering the students' personalities and potential. With this mindset, teachers can realistically accomplish what they intend to present, and that is all that matters.

In preparation for a scheduled evaluation, please make sure that your lesson plan is completely full with varied activities in which there is a lot of interaction between you and the students. In this way, your lesson plan should go very well.

For the actual class period of the scheduled observation by your administrator, please take a nice, big, deep breath to relax. If need be, please do the same several times during his or her visit. Students usually will behave a little bit better than they normally do, thus lessening the chances of discipline problems taking place. Also, the administrator will typically sit in the back of the classroom, thus allowing teachers to focus on the students more readily.

It is best to begin the class as it is normally done. This will ease a lot of tension for all concerned. It is also best to only focus on the students and not to focus on the administrator because the focus needs to be the students and their education. It does not matter at the moment what he or she is writing because they are reference notes that generally will be discussed in your postobservation meeting. Interaction with the students in informative, enlightening discussions will increase their education and will be looked upon highly by the students and by the observing administrator.

At the end of the class, please be sure to sum up what was discussed and to ask questions of the students. This may also be an appropriate time to inform them or to remind them about any homework for the next school day.

After the students have left the class and if the administrator is still present, please thank him or her for attending. While it is his or her duty to evaluate teachers, expressing gratitude adds a better bond between the two of you.

If the administrator has left prior to the end of class or if he or she leaves as the students leave, please express your gratitude to him or her when it is possible. Again, it will show that you appreciate his or her attendance and evaluation of the classroom that particular day.

Along with the administrative evaluation process, the district may also require a certain set number of specific goals or objectives for the school year. They typically can consist of how well the students have done on certain quizzes, tests, and/or projects. In the event your district does this, please formulate these goals well into the first semester so that your students will be familiar as to what your expectations are and so that your students will then have acquired better study habits. The end result can be that the goals hopefully will be achieved.

Once the students are prepared for these particular graded assignments and once they have completed them, please do your best to collect the data soon thereafter in order to determine how well the goals were reached so that this administrative task is complete for one of the goals for the year. It may mean having to ultimately ask the students to return their graded assignments for appropriate recordkeeping. Then you will not have to be concerned with this paperwork later on or close to the time that the results of your goals or objectives must be turned in.

Toward the end of the school year, there will be a final meeting to discuss the overall results of your teaching shown by the observations and all of the achieved or not achieved goals or objectives of the year.

When it comes to student achievement and goals or objectives, if the students have met the desired levels you have formulated, congratulations. If they did not meet the expectations, it needs to be realistically reevaluated as to how there could have been more success. Then again, it could be just the quality of students that particular year in those particular classes. Each class of students will be unique in their own way, thus making it either easier or more challenging to achieve one's goals or objectives.

When teachers do their best to complete their goals or objectives in a satisfactory manner, that is all that counts, and the administration will evaluate the dedication and the overall performance in order to determine whether or not teachers are to be rehired for the next school year, if teachers are in their first or second year. Of course, the district needs to take into account its financial status before permitting teachers to return the following school year.

If the teachers are tenured, if the district expectations are met, and if the district is financially stable, the teachers' assignment for the next school year is probably going to be secure.

There are two different perspectives about the evaluation procedure and goal setting. They can be viewed as being very critical or negative because teachers may be afraid that the administration will be looking for all of the procedures in class that can be undermined and/or that can be interpreted as being major flaws. Of course, there may be some positive comments stated, but the overall evaluation will be less than desirable. In turn, with enough critical reports, teachers can fear that they may lose their jobs.

On the other hand, these procedures can be viewed as being positive and helpful tools to validate or to improve what is going on in the classroom. Many teachers welcome administrators into their classrooms because it is a great way for administrators to get out of their offices and other assigned duties so that they can see how classes are being instructed, to determine how well students are learning, and to observe how well students are cooperating. Of course, there may be some constructive observations as to how the class could be managed better, but the overall evaluation will be very positive.

Many teachers are basically relieved when the administrative evaluation process is completed so that they do not have to worry about it until the next time. Whether the administrative evaluation process turns out to be a complete waste of time or a valid experience, it is a necessary analysis to determine how well teaching is taking place and how well the students are learning and behaving and to justify the employment of the teachers.

Another form of evaluation that is less threatening than the administrative evaluation process is when and if one teacher wishes to invite another teacher from one's own department to observe during preparation periods in order to give feedback. Since this teacher knows what it is like to be a teacher nowadays and knows how to teach the subject, it probably will be easier to relate to him or her, and there may be some actual value to his or her opinions and suggestions, even more so than the administrator-in-charge. This informal observation process is typically not part of any official evaluation that an administrator utilizes.

Perhaps teachers can also reverse their roles so that the observers can become the observed in order to give appropriate feedback. Who knows? There may be new techniques that you may want to incorporate. At any rate, it is your choice.

Another form of evaluation to be considered is a student evaluation of the teacher. If there is such a form already in place, you may wish to utilize it. If not, doing research at a bookstore or online could be helpful. In this way, the very persons whom you are helping can share their feedback as to what is being experienced in the classroom environment. If the students are mature enough for this tool, great. If the students would misuse this tool or if they would see this as a way to mock or to degrade, then it would be best not to include this manner of evaluation.

If students evaluate the classroom in a constructive, mature manner, this information is very valuable and can be helpful as to what is being accomplished and/or which issues may be present. It truly can be a great reflective tool that can show students that teachers do appreciate student input and that input can be considered, if the ideas have merit.

No matter what evaluation forms are mandatory or voluntary, the teacher is the final judge as to which ideas are worthy of consideration. It would be best to always remember that evaluation tools are judgments based on observations at specific times only. Thus, please consider the positive evaluations as validating one's teaching style. A teacher can be totally happy with the results of all of his or her hard work.

Please consider the so-called negative evaluations as possible roads for improvement. If it is only a person's critical opinion due to his or her negative personality, please consider the source. If the criticism is credible and worthy of consideration, fine. If there are many critical evaluations about your effectiveness, how about looking at it as a way to improve for the sake of the students?

If you disagree with the administrator's evaluation, you have the right to disagree, and there is nothing wrong with that. True, there can be disappointment by thinking that the evaluation's results are unfair. That is natural. How about taking a nice, big, deep breath under these circumstances, and how about reflecting on what has been stated? In turn, it is best to objectively reflect on the value of what has been stated and to make any appropriate changes, if it is believed that the negative evaluation may be justified.

On a schoolwide basis, there can be annual testing taking place at specific times of the year. For the sake of the school and its funding, please do the best to prepare your students to succeed. There probably are many techniques to motivate students already set in place by the teachers and by the administration, although if you do think of something worthy of consideration in order to assist the school's goal, please be sure to share the idea with an administrator.

Frankly, there is too much emphasis placed on testing, which only results in teaching to the test while there is consequently less focus placed on the actual learning and the application of the studied material. There needs to be a mind shift about testing because it is a way to determine how well students are learning. The results will be published and compared to other schools in your area along with comparisons with similar schools in the state and possibly the nation. So it is important to accentuate the value of these tests to the students by saying they can compare themselves from one year to the next. Perhaps some kind of reward can be given for taking it and for improvement.

CHAPTER EIGHT

~

Utilizing Available Resources

There truly are many resources available so that teaching is enhanced.

There may be computers in the classroom with Internet connections; however, teachers need to be on the alert that the students focus on appropriate websites that pertain to their studies. Constant monitoring of students on the Internet is important so that they remain on task.

The library has a multitude of resources for learning for students. The librarian is extremely knowledgeable as to how to obtain information from books instead of always on the Internet like students seem to prefer.

The computer lab and its specialist can be another great way to allow students and teachers to link to the Internet for various projects. Of course, when utilizing the computer lab, teachers again need to monitor the students' use of the Internet for the appropriate websites purposed for their studies and projects.

If and when there are adult aides who work with you, you are in a great position to acquire a lot of assistance for individual students or in small groups. It is important to know the academic strengths of these adult aides In turn, your lesson plans can be designed to allow adult aides to give quality, individual attention to students who need more attention and who may feel less inhibited in small groups.

This is not to say that you and these students should rely upon the adult aides because students still need to be involved in the classroom situation as much as possible. It is just that they need more time and more individual help to become better acquainted with the material that is being presented to the rest of the class, and it may be difficult when you have a big class.

It is important to receive input from the adult aides in order to develop individual lesson plans so that the adult aides will be able to assist these particular students. Another approach would be that if the adult aides are educated in the subject matter, they can utilize their own creativity to work with these students with the same material that is being learned in the classroom at the same time. If so, the adult aides need to get your permission because you are in charge of the total education of your students.

Ideally, if these adult aides could work with these particular students in another room, they would be less distracted. If not, being in a corner of your classroom would be the next possible solution.

Please be sure to find out how well these particular students are understanding the information from the adult aides on a daily basis. Of course, this does mean a little bit more time and more work on your part, but it can ultimately help the students in question to learn better.

It is advisable that the adults aides do not correct graded assignments because you as the teacher are the final indicator as to how much has been accomplished by these students, and it is important for you to be totally aware of what academic grade they deserve and how to justify it, if necessary.

Another great resource for you to utilize is the community of specialists, like reading and speech therapists. Due to limited funding, they may not be as plentiful as previously. Yet they certainly can be instrumental in the development of your students, if they have been diagnosed in order to receive this extra attention. Inevitably, it will help them in their education. Please be forewarned that it would mean taking them out of your classroom at various times, but they can easily catch up.

Mentor teachers are extremely valuable individuals who have the ability to help new teachers perfect their instructional methods along with being guides on the side. Each school district and each state will have its own methods of allowing mentor teachers to work with new teachers. They can certainly be very beneficial in their reflection of what is going on in the new teachers' classroom. Should you be interested in the process and in the selection of mentors, discussion will take place in a subsequent chapter.

There will be those instances in which you will be needing a substitute teacher. In preparation for that eventuality, it is a good idea to print up a blank lesson plan as to what you typically do at the beginning of the class, like taking care of attendance. It is also important to include what is considered appropriate behavior and what is inappropriate behavior. In the event the students misbehave, please provide the substitute teacher with a specific procedure to follow.

Then please allow enough space so that you can add specific information as to what the substitute teacher needs to instruct the students to complete.

One oftentimes overlooked resource that can be available for you is retired teachers. They have had a wealth of different experiences. If you are familiar with any of them particularly in your field of study and if you believe they are receptive to questions, they too can be your mentors; however, please do not frequently ask questions because they wish to fulfill their life experiences, especially after having served as teachers already. Moderation of the frequency of questions is the key.

One possible resource for you could be your students' parents or guardians, if you know of their knowledge of a particular subject. Should they have the time and the inclination, perhaps, they could work with you in order to give a presentation to your students with the approval of the administration. In this way, students will get another perspective of the subject matter, and they will more than likely be very cooperative and very respectful. Under these circumstances, the students should take good notes so that it can be a useful class session in the overall knowledge of the subject matter.

Another possible resource is student aides. Invariably, there are twelfth-grade students who will have completed all of their classes for graduation by the end of their eleventh grade due to taking summer school classes and independent study (which will be discussed later in this book). They need to fill in their schedule with a fairly easy class. So they may ask some teachers with whom they feel comfortable whether they can use student aides during their senior year. Another way students may sign up to become potential aides is with their counselor. In turn, the counselor can find out which teachers need student aides.

A teacher's aide can be helpful on a regular basis to photocopy materials, alphabetize papers, and do some general errands, which can help you focus more on your students' education instead.

When and if you do have student aides, it is advisable for them not to correct student work. Again, your position as the teacher is the final determiner of the progress and the final determiner of student grades. Besides, this information really is confidential.

Educational books located at local bookstores and libraries can be of benefit. If your local bookstores have websites, searches can be made in order to find out which resources will be very helpful. You can browse through the books in order to see if they can meet your educational needs. Also, any desired books may be able to be purchased online, thus saving you time and gas. If you so desire, just going to the bookstore to browse through the actual books can be that much more meaningful in order to know the specific contents and the possible benefits for you.

Another wealth of information can be attained from educational workshops offered by colleges, universities, and companies related to your subject matter and related to classroom management. It would be best to check your mailboxes for advertisements as well as to check with your department chairs for possible monies that might be available to attend conferences. Please also consider attending any workshop that deals with students' self-esteem and how these techniques can be utilized for student learning.

Your local teachers' unions typically deal with monetary and job-related issues. The state teachers' unions typically deal with political issues and offer conferences. Educational organizations such as the National Education Association (www.nea.org), the American Federation of Teachers (www.aft.org), and the Phi Delta Kappa organization (www.pdkintl.org) offer a multitude of workshops and conventions that can be very useful.

By having access to the Internet, you can acquire ideas about your subject by doing Google searches along with checking other websites that you may know about already.

There may be a league of high schools available in your state. For example, in California, there is the California League of High Schools at www.clhs .net, which offers a multitude of resources, support, and conferences that can be very helpful for you.

It would be a good idea to check www.teacherspayteachers.com because there are many teachers worldwide who have knowledge from the kindergarten level through the university level in every conceivable subject. It is quite a wealthy resource of information from which a lot can be learned and from which you can possibly earn money, and the membership fee is nominal.

Another great resource on the Internet is www.curriki.org, which has the same format as the previous website but is totally free without any money to be earned and without any charges.

There are some social websites that can be useful. Teachers can look at www.youtube.com for different subject areas. Another avenue to possibly pursue is www.facebook.com, which includes different teacher groups that can be helpful due to the ideas that other active and retired teachers share. There are also different teacher groups on the website www.myspace.com.

English teachers could utilize www.bookrags.com, which consists of many books summarized and analyzed chapter by chapter in depth. This website can be very helpful for both students and teachers, and the fees are very nominal.

If you have a webcam for your computer or if you want to buy a webcam to attach to your computer, downloading the application from www.skype .com can be very helpful so that you can communicate with literally anyone throughout the world, whether they are friends, relatives, or other professionals. This video calling is totally free of charge on the Internet. You just need to coordinate the time when you and the other person wish to talk with one another. If video conference calling with two or more people and/or voice mails are desired, there are charges for these services.

A family member or a friend could be possibly helpful. If you feel comfortable with him or her to discuss school matters, he or she can certainly be helpful and objective. Should you do this, please consider not disclosing any names or information about people out of respect and confidentiality of your students and their parents or guardians.

Ultimately, you are the final authority as to which resources of information are worthy of consideration and are useful based on your classes. Also, by effectively utilizing adult aides and student aides, more successes in the classroom environment can be achieved.

CHAPTER NINE

~

Working with Your Colleagues

As you grew up, while there were probably many times of agreement with your parents or guardians, relatives, and friends, there were also probably times of disagreement. Adults were probably respected and perceived as the important authority, not to be confronted and not to be argued with, while friends of your own age were easier to either agree with or to disagree with.

Now that you are older and more cognizant of your world, there will be many times when you will agree about different issues with your colleagues so that there will be progress. These particular times are very easy to deal with due to a general consensus.

Nevertheless, since your perspective can be different compared to the other people of your school's department or within the school, there will be times of mild to strong disagreement. That is just how human nature is. We all cannot think the same way all the time. Of course, there are rules that need to be followed because that is what the district and school policies expect of the entire school community.

So what can be done when you adamantly oppose a decision? Please mentally prepare yourself with some notes that support your point of view. When meeting with your colleagues, please breathe deeply before beginning to say anything to the other people involved in order to feel calmer.

Your ability to listen well may result in them listening to your opposing ideas carefully. That can be helpful now and in future discussions. By tactfully saying: "I understand your opinion, but I respectfully disagree," you are actively listening and also declaring a different sense of the situation. Also, your appreciation can be given to them by just saying: "Thank you for listening to my point of view." By showing respect and by showing appreciation of what they are saying, you help them have that much more respect and that much more appreciation for you, even though there still may be different perspectives.

If there is still no resolution and if there is a need to resolve the situation, just delaying any final decision by a day or two can possibly result in another meeting. When all are rested, it is possible that there can be some form of compromise in which everyone can agree on a specific way to deal with the issue. It is possible that it might be actually better than your original proposal and the original proposal of the other person. More time may be needed, or there may be no resolution whatsoever. It all depends on how major or minor the issue may be.

Here is an example. Let's say that your department wants to change to a new textbook. You may like a particular one while your colleagues may prefer another one instead. It is important to share your opinion so that your voice is heard. After all, you are integral part of the process. It is also important for others to share their perspectives. Everyone can thus understand the advantages and the disadvantages of the textbook in question.

Afterward, whatever decision is finally made, everyone needs to agree, if at all possible. When all is said and done, everyone needs to be satisfied with whichever textbook is going to be the most helpful for teaching and for student learning.

Let's say there have already been healthy discussions on whatever the issue may be, but they have resulted in confrontations where there are ill feelings, and you have lost in this argument. Sometimes, you win, and, sometimes, you lose. We cannot always get our own way. We will have times when we are satisfied with the ultimate decision. We do live in a democracy in which the will of the majority of the people is normally accepted. In other words, you both need to agree to disagree. The final decision needs to be not only respected but also followed in order to continue the trust among all colleagues involved.

If your department teachers are receptive, it is best to have a teacher available after school Mondays through Thursdays for students who need extra help. Fridays are not desirable due to the fact that students and teachers prefer to begin their weekends early. All of you could determine a rotating schedule to not overburden any particular teacher.

Since teachers want to give a quality education to their students, some students simply need more individual time with teachers so that they can have their questions answered. This accessibility to teachers can truly benefit the individual students to improve their understanding and their grades.

Agreements, disagreements, and compromises need to take place for the benefit of the school environment. Also, mutual respect needs to be maintained among all colleagues.

~

CHAPTER TEN

Working with Students' Parents/Guardians

If one considers what a jury does in a court room, they listen objectively to the testimony given. They deliberate and do the best they can to determine their decision.

In the classroom, you are the judge and the jury by observing and listening to what is going on with students while still trying to be focused on teaching the subject material. If the situation is such that you cannot perform your duties in an orderly process due to some sort of student disruption, action needs to take place. A minor disturbance only requires discussing the situation with the student one on one or looking at him or her, indicating that he or she needs to focus better or there will be consequences, like detention or a phone call to the parents or guardians.

When there is a situation in which a student is being majorly disruptive, being calm, firm, and fair will show that the teacher is in charge in the classroom right away. By being calm, the teacher is more in control. With firmness and fairness, the student involved will understand that there are certain teacher expectations. By being assertive without being overpowering, there is less of a chance of reacting with anger to the situation, and the class's education and maintenance of order can be restored. While this is easier said than done, calmness, firmness, fairness, and assertiveness with time and with practice can be ultimately achieved a majority of the time.

When there is a disruption with inappropriate behavior disturbing the educational process, it may warrant moving the student to another side of the class where there will be fewer disturbances. The student might need to stand outside the classroom to calm down. The student may need to be sent to the administration office or to the counselor's office. It all depends on the nature and the severity of the situation in order to determine which of these actions is best suited under the circumstances.

When all of the above has taken place and if there is still no improvement in the young adult's behavior, a parent-student-teacher conference needs to take place. It would be a good idea to explain to the student what your intentions are. It is not a threat. It is not a promise. It just means that everything has been done to encourage and to persuade him or her to improve in terms of cooperation, and he or she has chosen not to behave. Thus, you have decided on the next logical step, to confer with all concerned. Of course, if there is a major, positive change and if there is better cooperation promised and practiced by the student, there is no need to continue with the following steps.

When everything has failed and when there is no determined difference by the student, it is then a good idea to call the parents or guardians, usually in the evening, in order to determine when everyone can meet at the school, if at all possible. The ideal situation is that one or ideally both of the parents or guardians can meet with you and the student at school with the counselor and perhaps even another administrator, if the situation is severe enough. It has that much more of a visual and emotional impact, especially for the student involved, when everyone can see one another, rather than just hearing voices over the phone and dealing with the issues in that manner.

If it is not in the realm of possibility to have a conference during the school day, it is a good idea to have this conference at a mutually acceptable time in the evening over the phone with the young adult on an extension phone or with everyone talking on a speaker phone. Thus, the student, the parents or guardians, and the teacher would be involved in this conversation.

Since there are all kinds of people, there are all kinds of parents or guardians who raise their young adults, usually in the best way they can. They usually can give love, support, protection, and care to them. They usually can feel a lot of pride for their children as they accomplish their goals and even surpass everybody's expectations, thus feeling so very proud of them and even idealizing them oftentimes. These particular parents or guardians can become very defensive about their young adults, if and when there is a problem that the student has.

These young adults also can relate one side of the issue to their parents, with them not knowing the full scope of the issue involved. Their parents may be able to listen to their young adults but may realize that there are always two sides, knowing the teacher may understand everything involved.

There are also a lot of parents who have devoted so much time and effort during the elementary school years and feel burned out. They can be very realistic to the point of being negative, feeling that they are not able to control their own young adults anymore and hoping for the best that the high school community can dramatically change their young adults' attitude. They believe that by the time their young adults are in high school, they need to become self-reliant and are responsible for their own actions. In essence, they have given up or have lost confidence in their own children, and they feel their young adults control the home.

In preparation for a conference in regard to behavior issues, it is a good idea to have notes prepared. These notes should include specific dates, specific actions by the students, and subsequent actions by you to improve the situation. Granted, it means a little more paperwork on your part, but it can be helpful and supportive for all concerned to recognize the extent of the situation.

When the conference takes place, it is valuable to take a big breath in order to feel calmer and less stressed. Please emphasize the fact that parents or guardians, the student, the administrator if present, and you as the teacher are the best team for the benefit of the student. It is best to talk with everyone with respect and with tact.

Please accentuate the positive of the student at first, emphasizing what he or she has done correctly. Then, instead of saying that he or she is fooling around so much, it may be more worthwhile to tactfully indicate the specific details of concern for this meeting. It may be said that he or she is capable of improving, if he or she clearly focuses totally on what needs to be done in class without being distracted or without being a distraction to others.

Also, it is important to state that fair, realistic expectations are for the benefit of all of your students, and you may want to delineate specific behaviors that are acceptable and those that are unacceptable.

Next, the student needs to address the issues involved. He or she can understandably become very defensive at that time. Yet his or her point of view truly deserves to be heard in its totality and respected.

Afterward, the parents or guardians need to state their opinions about the situation at hand.

From this point on, there needs to be more discussion. There may be issues that you will not have known about that can explain the discipline issue. Nevertheless, it is important to tactfully state that this explanation does not legitimize the bad behavior. There needs to be a way to change the young adult's behavior so that there can be better communication between you as the teacher and the student and so that he or she can focus on learning instead of the bad behavior, and the rest of the class deserves to learn as well as possible without disruptions of any form whatsoever.

The last expectation of this type of meeting is that there is mutual respect to hopefully alleviate these discipline issues from happening again.

Upon the completion of the conference, please thank all concerned for their time and please state your optimism and hope that the student can improve from now on. It may be a good idea to mention that the parents or guardians will hear from you within two weeks to indicate what kind of progress has been made by the student in terms of behavior and in terms of his or her grade. In this way, the student involved knows that he or she is accountable for improving behaviorally and perhaps even academically.

If and when you have parent-student-teacher-administrative meetings in regard to grades, it is extremely important to have up-to-date grades, whether it be from a computer's grading program or from the gradebook. With all of this data, the results of the homework, quizzes, tests, and projects can be shared with the young adult, the parents or guardians, the counselor, and maybe even an administrator with photocopies. Please emphasize that all grades are earned and that they are not given. It would then be best to find out what the objection may be and to specifically detail all the grades so that everyone will understand how the overall grade was determined.

Should there be a difference in the specific grades, it would be best to resolve where the problem might be so that the correct grade could be assessed.

If the young adult is struggling in understanding the information of the class, methods of how to study and where to get help need to be suggested. Please suggest that the student reorganizes his or her time for outside responsibilities so that there is a better focus on learning.

It might also be worthy to mention that the teacher is only a guide while the young adult is the one responsible for any learning taking place. Also, please indicate when you are available for extra individual help. In this way, the lines of communication are open to all concerned.

Please suggest that the student shows his or her parents or guardians the assigned homework for the next school day on a daily basis. If the school has a homework service online, it is a good idea for all concerned, namely the student and parents or guardians, to find out the name of the website and to find out about assignments and grades not only for your class but also for the other classes.

If there are written assignments, the parents or guardians can check the homework to make sure that they look complete, even if the parents or guardians do not know anything about the subject. If they have knowledge in this subject area, please suggest that they review them in detail for accuracy.

If it is an assignment that only requires studying and the student says that it has been done, please suggest that the parents or guardians ask some general questions to their young adult based on the material. This will help the student involved to know and to understand the material, and this will help the parents or guardians to know that their young adults know the information. Afterward, it is best for them to quiz the young adult again for comprehension.

More than likely, the young adult will not like these suggestions; however, this approach needs to be done so that the information is known better and in order to improve the chances of success.

A weekly grade check to evaluate the progress of their young adult may be advisable so that these parents or guardians are informed, if it is not available online. It is also good to have so that the teachers can write any comments in terms of any improvement or any concerns of those particular weeks.

If these conferences are for both behavior and academic reasons, it is desirable to be that much more prepared with all of the student information discussed in this chapter. Please mention to all concerned that when the student misbehaves, he or she does not listen and will not be informed. In turn, he or she needs to be held accountable for any lack of progress.

Parents or guardians are an integral part of the learning process and need to be involved. With your care and with your thorough accounting of student behavior and grades, everyone can be accurately aware of what has been done and what needs to be modified.

CHAPTER ELEVEN

~

Time Is of the Essence!

In order to attain and to maintain success with your students daily, time is of the essence. In a manner of speaking, the teacher needs to be like Phileas Fogg, the forever devoted person concerned with time in Jules Verne's *Around the World in Eighty Days.*

In the teaching world, you have become cognizant of managing time. A determined amount of time is needed to complete a certain amount of objectives in each of your classes each day. Firsthand experiences can be learned as far as which classes are able to handle whatever amount of material.

If too little information and practice are covered for your classes, there will be extra time at the end of your classes. Under these circumstances, planning needs to be revised in order to cover more material.

Thus, developing lesson plans is vitally important to be realistic about, so that you accomplish what you design. How many minutes will it take for all activities, whether it be a lecture, a video, a group discussion, a project presented to the class, a quiz, or a test, for example? With time and practice, you can judge how much time is needed to complete the day's objective or objectives.

In the event you are a new teacher and in the event you wish to have more specific advice based on the subjects you teach, it is important to consult with fellow teachers as to what they have experienced with lesson planning in regard to the specifics of your subject area.

There are always variables to consider. Students could enter a classroom first period on a Monday, and it seems as though they are still asleep. You could be teaching this very same class fifth period, and your students may be very alert.

Classes can be rather slow in grasping a concept, or they can be able to apply their learned concept almost immediately. You could be dealing with some unruly students, which makes it especially challenging to educate an entire class. Even if you do have so-called perfect or better-achieving students, always be aware of how much time is allotted for each of your classes.

In terms of the length of the school day, there are many high schools that have the normal six- or seven-period day with the traditional school year in place. The teachers may have several preparations, but they will have the standard five to seven classes to teach every day.

There are benefits for the teachers in that if they like to deal with a variety of students each day, this will suit their needs, especially if they have students who tend to be quite rambunctious or have discipline problems.

There are benefits for the students because they are able to have a variety of classes with different teachers and possibly many different students. Students get more physical exercise by walking from class to class. If the students do not necessarily get along well with the teachers, at least it is only for a short period of time each day. Students may experience less stress in terms of learning compared to other types of school schedules because they have more time over a period of an entire school year.

For coaches and for band instructors, the traditional school schedule is useful and may be the same as other high schools in the area for games and band reviews, for example.

For parents or guardians, this traditional high school time frame is useful. They can plan their schedules and vacations accordingly, and they are accustomed to that due to their own experience with traditional school schedules.

There are many high schools that have a modified, traditional school year in which high schools are in session for approximately six weeks and are not in session for two or three weeks.

This can be good and bad. It can be good so that the teachers and the students are able to focus on the material for a specific time period, knowing that they will have some free time in contrast to the traditional school schedule. It can be bad especially from the teachers' perspective in terms of trying to always regain the students' enthusiasm and retention of the subject when there is a schedule of this nature.

Coaches and band instructors need to work with other high schools in the area that may still have the traditional schedule, thus requiring coaches and athletes to participate even during times in which there is no school. If the other high schools have the same schedule, it is then easier for scheduling purposes.

For parents or guardians, this can be a nightmarish situation because if their young adults are not involved in a sport or band and if both parents or guardians are working, they need to formulate their own plans to make sure that their young adults are occupied with enough to do, even if they may have some school homework and/or even if they may work on a part-time basis.

There are many high schools that have found a form of block schedule to be very useful for them. The block schedule usually consists of four classes that meet each day for approximately ninety minutes with the standard morning and lunch breaks during a semester. In these four classes, the teachers cover all of the material of one year in one semester, which is similar to the college environment.

For those students who intend to go to college and if they are taking advanced placement classes, teachers and students need to work together as much as possible to prepare for their advanced placement tests, which might not necessarily take place during a time that the students have these classes.

There are some distinct advantages to the block schedule in that students get a concentrated education for half the time of the school year. They can possibly delve into the subjects in that much more depth for ninety minutes each school day without having to worry as much about the time constraint of a typical fifty- to fifty-five-minute class period schedule of the traditional high school.

In contrast to the traditional school year in which students typically have a total of seven classes, students attending a high school with the block schedule will have studied a total of eight classes in a given school year.

If the students are well behaved, then this is ideal. If the students are discipline problems, the teachers can truly dread having these particular students for an extended period of time of ninety minutes. If the students or the teachers do not necessarily like one another that much, at least a semester is a lot better than a full year.

If the students seem to understand the material very well, great. If the students cannot seem to master the material very well and if there is a limited amount of time to study, namely one semester, these students may become lost by not understanding the subject matter. Under these circumstances, teachers suggest that these students see them before or after school to get extra help, to work with a "study buddy," and/or to become involved in a peer tutoring program, if available.

When students are absent for one or more days, this can become a night-marish situation for them and for their teachers because they will have a lot of notes and a lot of homework to complete from the days missed and will also have to contend with the new material presented and new homework when they return.

No matter what type of schedule your high school may have, there are definite advantages and disadvantages for the teachers, for the students, for the parents or guardians, for the coaches, and for the band instructors. It requires flexibility by all concerned. The bottom line of it all is that you as the teacher need to teach to the best of your ability based on your school's schedule so that your students are able to have a better understanding of the material presented to them, and it is important to manage the classroom environment so that the students are cooperative.

Speaking about timing, if you were to seriously consider leaving in the middle of the school year due to pure frustration for whatever reason, you would need to understand the possible repercussions. Your administration will not look too kindly upon this decision. Your administration may have a challenge hiring a replacement.

Once the replacement teacher arrives, it will be difficult for him or her in terms of discipline because it is almost like starting a new year and the students may want to take advantage of the situation. That may not be a concern for you under these circumstances; however, what you need to take into account is the education of the students themselves and how they will be affected. They may even have several substitute teachers who may not know as much information as you.

When and if you were to seek a teaching assignment somewhere else, that school administration would want to know where you had been teaching. Then it is very well possible that you could receive a poor recommendation, thus limiting your chances of getting a new teaching job. Even if you decide to leave the teaching field, any future employer will wish to find out where you had been employed, thus not looking too good for you because the best interest of the previous employer was not considered.

Your frustration dealing with your misbehaving students may be a major factor for wanting to quit teaching during the school year. Yet, with time, patience, and practice of new discipline techniques learned from fellow staff members and from classroom management workshops, you may be able to reach a majority of your students. Of course, this is easier said than done, but it can be done.

There may be issues with your fellow teachers and/or with your admin-istration that you simply cannot tolerate for different reasons, like their attitude and/or their work ethics. Under these circumstances, please remember that your focus is your students' education. When having that mindset and if you get along with a majority of your students, perhaps your fellow teachers and/or your administration can be viewed as a necessary nuisance. In turn, it would be to your advantage to limit working with them as much as possible and really focus a majority of your time and your effort on the purpose of being employed—teaching students your subject.

If you decide to shorten your stay in education to only one or several years, this is a very difficult decision to make. After all, you have already prepared yourself to become a teacher with many years devoted for this specific purpose. Please be sure to think it over a great deal as well as to learn different techniques from different teachers and workshops. Perhaps you can become encouraged again to want to remain in education.

If you are absolutely certain you wish to leave the teaching profession due to pure frustration about so many factors, please remain until the end of the school year for the sake of the students who need to learn all of the information they need to know. There is a distinct personal advantage in that when wishing to apply for future employment; it can be said that you have taught at that high school for so many complete years, and when and if they wish to call or write your high school administration for professional references, they can evaluate you accordingly.

How we utilize time in our classrooms is especially important, and our planning will help to inform our students thoroughly. Hopefully, it will also be an enjoyable experience for all in which they can be challenged as well, thus minimizing discipline problems.

~

CHAPTER TWELVE

The Teacher's Perspective about the Classes

When there are good teaching days, it seems as though life will go rather smoothly. When there are the so-called bad or challenging teaching days, it seems as though nothing seems to go well at all. It definitely takes a lot of emotional strength to be in front of the class when something is bothering you. Under these circumstances, it is important to do the best possible to change your mindset for the sake of the class.

So what do you do to change your mindset? Of course, everyone is able to answer this question in different ways. If you have found something that works, great. It will make your day that much better, and it will also help your students that much more.

Here are some suggestions that may help for those days that seem intolerable:

1. On the way to school, how about putting on some upbeat music that is considered inspirational?
2. Please do not put on the news to hear about the latest crises in the world.
3. Please drive a different way to school because you will have to think differently, which hopefully will entice you to feel different as well.
4. When you have a day off, how about going to an amusement park to spend a day there to act like the kid who lives within you by riding rollercoasters and bumper cars and doing everything else you enjoy there?

5. How about exercising rigorously to release any tension that may be building up?

6. What about going to a movie or renting a DVD in order to escape from it all for a couple of hours?

When teachers have a positive mindset, their jobs will be a labor of love, the hardest job that they will ever love, along with an appropriate focus and goal in mind.

When it is the very first day of school, your new students enter into the classroom. They seem to be oddly quiet. They do not know what to expect, and many of them are probably new. Thus, there can be an air of anticipation and apprehension by the students and you.

With time, the classroom's personalities will begin to appear, and the students can become a joy to work with, a challenge, and/or "just there," meaning they might not even want to be enrolled in the class, let alone attending school.

Of course, dealing with a class filled with a dynamic, intellectually inspiring bunch of students can be any teacher's dream. The teacher can feel genuine excitement to see them because they are eager to attend and ready to learn. They are inspirational and glowing stars for the school year and possible leaders of our future society.

It is interesting to note that this scenario can become a self-fulfilling prophecy. The teacher is excited to present creative, dynamic ideas to inspired students, which can breed that much more excitement in them.

Nevertheless, even the so-called top-notch students are human. Although they seemingly act more mature, they can and will misbehave. There are certainly some who feel that they are so smart that they know everything. They feel that just being themselves and being in an advanced class will qualify them automatically to earn the highest possible grades; they believe that they are superior in their intelligence and perhaps even much more popular than the rest of the so-called average and so-called below average students.

Although the better classes are usually better in terms of their grades, their behavior, and their attitude, they too have their issues, and they can be perhaps spoiled. All of these students need to learn and to accept the fact that every grade is earned and not given whatsoever. If they have devoted enough time and effort into their work, the chances are they will earn a higher grade; however, if they put in a minimal amount of work and do not have the complete understanding of the material, their grade will reflect that.

In contrast to the highly motivated students, a lot of teachers encounter a lot more students who are supposedly average or below average. These students oftentimes may feel confused and frustrated for many different reasons, thus acting out in different ways. They may act out by not doing their homework. They may not do well on their assignments. Their attitudes will reflect their unwillingness to participate or their desire to create problems for themselves, for their fellow students, and for you. So what do you do in these situations?

While their individual issues do seem paramount to them, a teacher's attitude can truly change them in so many important ways. Before the students enter the classroom, if a teacher dreads the fact that he or she will have to tolerate them, it will be a dreadful class session. It can again become a self-fulfilling prophecy.

When a teacher consistently and genuinely shows kindness and respect toward them, that may result in them being kind and respectful. When a teacher utilizes humor about one's subject, some tension is apt to be alleviated.

When a teacher shows genuine confidence in the fact that they can learn their subject with time, practice, patience, tact, and flexibility, they can feel more inclined to work with a teacher and to the best of their ability. In turn, they may actually create fewer problems for themselves, for others around them, and for the teacher.

All students of different degrees of intelligence and of attitude deserve and need encouragement when they do not do well, and they deserve and need praise when they have met or even surpassed their own expectations. In this way, a teacher can change an attitude from self-dejection to self-worth, from a negative perspective about the world to a positive attitude of excitement and eagerness to learn, thus enhancing the chances for success in the classroom and, quite possibly, in their future as well.

Jaime Escalante from California understood the students from East Los Angeles whose outside lives consisted of drugs, alcohol, gangs, murders, and single family homes. The students' attitudes were very poor, and he was able to inspire them by giving the perspective that their situation outside the school did not define who they were and their potential. He was able to make a definite, positive difference with a majority of his students in fantastic ways so that they could surpass their actual existence in order to become positive, intelligent young adults. The movie *Stand and Deliver* summarizes his successes.

When teachers can promote a sense of trust and support and instill joy into their love of learning of the subject, students can have a better chance of learning the information and feeling excited about life. In turn, students learn how to trust teachers who genuinely care about them. They know that life can be challenging, but it can also be a joyous ride, a life worth living, that there is hope, and that there is a future for them with wonderful possibilities when they work.

Accentuating their strengths while being realistic, tactful, and encouraging about where they need to improve, teachers and students are then working in unison with the purpose of learning in a positive environment. It is interesting if a teacher has a student who consistently is a problem, that if a teacher gives him or her a compliment, it is actually difficult to accept because it may be easier to accept a criticism rather than a positive comment. Generally speaking, it can make a difference in the relationship with that student when he or she feels that the teacher is being caring, although it all depends upon how receptive and willing the student in question is.

Along with accentuating the positive, students need to learn to be self-reliant and self-accountable in terms of their behavior, in terms of their learning, and in terms of their grades. In turn, they will become that much more mature and more appreciative of what is being done with them and on behalf of them. They can thus attain self-confidence, which will help them now and in the future.

Students need to learn that they need to help one another, not only in their personal lives but also helping each other in their classes, thus reducing the selfish nature of a lot of students. In turn, this will help when they are older and they are reliant on others in their personal and professional relationships.

Assigning group projects where each group member is interdependent upon the others can help them appreciate one another better. There is a lot of controversy about the worthiness of group work because there are naturally students who wish to be proactive while others are simply reliant on others to do the work. Nevertheless, even those students who rely upon the proactive ones can learn. As for resolving this issue, this oftentimes needs to be taken care of by the students themselves. In this respect, peer pressure can be very helpful.

Teachers need to show them their "humanness" while still being the teachers, which is a delicate act to accomplish. When something is funny about the subject and it is appropriate, students can relate more easily. They need to see that it can be a lot of fun, but it also consists of a lot of work. Teachers can loosen up by laughing when appropriate along with being focused on learning. In turn, the unmotivated students with low self-esteem may possibly rise from their personal issues to want to laugh, to feel better about themselves, and to want to learn in the classroom.

If teachers are so inclined, it can be simply fun to participate in rallies, showing their fun side, that they can make light of the serious nature of school, to do something out of the ordinary. Students can have a good laugh and realize that teachers do have a good sense of humor. Of course, if students subsequently act as though they can be mischievous as a result of teachers having participated in a comical way in a rally, teachers need to become that much firmer to reestablish control in the classroom in order to restore a learning environment where respect is demonstrated all the time.

Please be aware of students' fads and current slang words. It does not mean to use them incessantly, because you are the adult; however, if you make reference to them as they pertain to your subject area and are appropriate for classroom use, your students might pay attention even more.

So your devotion and your enthusiasm for your subject are extremely important for success in your classroom. Your attitude and your confidence can make all the difference in the world for your students. Your perspective of them can most certainly affect their lives in a positive fashion.

CHAPTER THIRTEEN

~

Mutual Respect

Along with doing one's best to have the appropriate perspective about students, another vital ingredient is mutual respect.

Mutual respect needs to be looked at from the point of view of the students. If you were now a student in your classroom, would having respect along with learning the information be important? You hopefully could respect the teacher with a secondary, extremely important hope that he or she would respect you as an individual and as a student for your abilities to learn.

So how does a teacher attain and maintain the ideal state of mutual respect? A teacher needs to know who the students are as individuals instead of massive numbers of bodies in the classroom.

What if a teacher were to consider students as young adults? Of course, they are young, but they are becoming more opinionated about the adult world. They are not little kids anymore. They are not adults; however, they are becoming more aware about what responsibility and accountability are, even though they may wish to live in denial about these life necessities oftentimes.

By treating them as young adults, teachers raise their consciousness as being more responsible and accountable for themselves. An interesting way for a teacher to accomplish this goal is to call them Mr., Miss, or Ms. Perhaps just doing that can result in them realizing that they are being treated more like adults, thereby improving the classroom atmosphere. If it is preferred to be less formal by simply calling them by their first names, so be it. Of course, it is desirable for mutual respect that they address a teacher as Mr., Miss, Mrs., or Ms. with his or her last name. A coach could choose either to be called "Coach" or "Coach" with the person's last name.

When a teacher listens intently to what students say, they will understand that a teacher cares. Acknowledging what they say by saying something to them gives them the respect they deserve. This can also be accomplished by a nod or a smile.

Students need to feel comfortable in agreeing and disagreeing with a teacher with tact and with consideration of his or her authority. In this way, students can be heard, even though they may not necessarily like the response.

If the disagreement has merit, a teacher needs to consider its importance and how to remedy the situation. This will provide the ground work for better mutual respect and fewer discipline problems.

Another important aspect to require in your classroom is proper manners. Nowadays, students oftentimes expect something to be done for them. They may have the philosophy that teachers are being paid to do their job, and manners can be disregarded.

A teacher may have to tactfully suggest that students use proper manners to obtain and maintain mutual respect. It is always considerate of people when they wish to have something done by someone else to genuinely say "please" along with the rationale for wanting something done. Of course, everyone needs to learn how to ask for something in a gentler, more respectful manner rather than demanding something.

It is important that students learn what gratitude is and to say "thank you" or "thanks" and that the other person says "You're welcome."

It is always considerate of people to genuinely say "excuse me" or "pardon me" when there is a need to do so, like bumping someone or interrupting someone accidentally.

It is important for a teacher to be considerate using these same words with students.

Consequently, there will be a much better environment in which there is that much more genuine politeness, which will help teachers, students, and their encounters with people from that point on.

It would be worthy to consider giving compliments to students whenever a teacher feels it is appropriate and genuine. When students are complimented individually and/or as a class for how they look, how they have improved academically, how they behaved so well, and how their attitude has changed for the better, a teacher might not necessarily see a reaction by the students because they may feel very surprised or they may feel slightly or very embarrassed; however, they will have listened. This can have subsequent positive results for the classroom atmosphere.

Let's face it. A teacher can like and dislike students based on interactions with them. Thus, it might be a challenge to try to use proper manners and kindness with those students who are disliked or a continuous nuisance. Please consider that deep down inside each student is the need to be liked and to be respected. When a teacher shows proper manners and kindness in a genuine fashion, he or she can truly form positive student behavior. If there is a major positive transformation, great. If there is no success whatsoever, it may take a longer period of time or not at all. It all depends upon the individual students, their life experiences, and their subsequent receptivity.

What can be especially helpful for mutual respect is hope. When giving hope to students, you can inspire them to want to achieve along with having a better positive self-concept. In turn, your students' response can possibly lead to better behaved classes.

There are those students who continuously refuse to accept any type of kindness, encouragement, praise, or hope. They will continuously discount any positive, caring ways by thinking: "Oh, I bet he or she is just saying that and really does not mean it." They may remain silent, or they may continually make degrading remarks criticizing themselves, their teachers, their fellow students, and anyone else. All you can do is to try your best to convince them that they are deserving of respect and hope for the best.

While a teacher instructs students in the best way possible, it is very important to try to be as acutely aware as possible as to any significant emotional problems which may be taking place for them. Their outlook on life might be so blemished or so severely damaged due to their own personal circumstances that they could need intensive counseling to deal with their issues. Please address the counselors-in-charge about what is happening about these students, if and when it becomes dramatically noticeable. Consequently, it is the counselors' job to discuss the matter more personally with the students involved.

Here is an example of a discipline problem in the classroom. Most of the students are attentive to what the teacher is doing, and they are following the directions. One student, however, is reading a magazine inside the text in the back of the class.

The teacher could go over and grab the magazine out of the student's hands which will result in forced compliance at that moment and attention by the rest of the class. The operative words are "forced compliance," because the teacher is changing current action, but not the future behavior. This can result in hostile feelings by the student, even if it is known that it was the wrong thing to do.

On the other hand, given this same scenario, the teacher can take a moment and go over to the student. The teacher can state the following in a nonaggressive manner: "You can continue choosing to read your magazine. Then, you will not learn and earn lower grades. You will also be assigned detention. Your citizenship grade will be reduced (if you assign citizenship grades at your school). The choice is yours. The responsibility is yours. So, please help yourself by paying attention to what we are doing now."

Granted, the student will feel probably embarrassed because of being put on the spot. Yet, the teacher is addressing the problem in a more constructive manner instead of in a dictatorial manner by physically removing the magazine from the student. The student will understand what is expected and that this behavior is a choice with consequences. Also, the student will hopefully make better decisions in the future as to how to cooperate and how to behave better with the end result of learning more. This approach is focused on the present behavior so that that action will hopefully not take place in the future.

If this situation continues, it is in the best interest again not to overreact with anger. It is probably better to again politely request not reading the magazine in the way that was explained. Then, after class is over, it is important to discuss the situation with the student. It may be an issue of boredom which could mean that the student needs to be challenged more by doing independent work. The student may be actually expressing boredom that the entire class is feeling, thus enlightening the teacher to incorporate different, better techniques. It may be a situation that there is an emotional issue and is really not reading the magazine whatsoever. Whatever is going on, there needs to be a discussion for the ultimate aim of a solution.

It is always imperative not to be hostile with students, whether it be verbally or physically. That will only create friction between the teacher and the students involved, thus decreasing mutual respect.

All one needs to do is to think about the consequences of verbal confrontations. Reacting with anger will not alleviate the situation. It will worsen the situation, instead. It is like adding fuel to the fire. It will not resolve the issue. While it is easier said than done, it is essential to assess the situation as calmly as possible.

Here is another example. A student confronts a teacher making an absurd accusation. A teacher could swear and make degrading remarks. On the other hand, a teacher could calmly state that the student's concerns will be addressed once he or she calms down. Hopefully, this will help. If not, being assertive and continuing being calm can help. Once calmness has been attained, then, there can be a discussion between the two of them.

If such confrontations take place during class, focusing on all the students' education needs to be the highest priority. A teacher could say that whatever concern the student has needs to take place before or after school. If the student is insistent on creating a scene during class, maintaining calmness and calling the administration need to be considered.

When there is physical aggression exhibited by placing one's hands on the students to correct misbehaviors, a teacher is jeopardizing his or her job. Also, by acting aggressively and violently toward students, a teacher may be placed on administrative leave, lose one's license to teach, be sued, and/or be arrested by the local police department.

So, it is best to calm down by taking a big, deep breath, no matter how hostile the students may be. It is easier said than done; however, it is to the teacher's advantage to act responsibly as the adult under these circumstances. It is best to act assertively by understanding calmly what the issue is with the students and to restore order, even if it means removing the students involved out of the classroom.

At first, especially when one is a new teacher, it might be difficult to practice this process of classroom management. This comes with time and experience. To quicken your discipline style and if monies are available, workshops about handling discipline situations can be very beneficial.

Nowadays, students hear swearing from different sources: television, movies, friends, and relatives. Consequently, students will follow these examples whenever they feel it is appropriate. While a teacher cannot forceably tell them not to swear, he or she can determine specific guidelines and consequences based on the high school's expectations. It is also exceedingly important to follow the high school's student conduct code very closely in order to establish appropriate behavior and appropriate talking.

Also, while a teacher may wish to swear at a situation in the classroom or with students, a teacher needs to consider different ways of expressing frustration without resorting to swearing. A teacher could say that what was written in a homework assignment was not the best, but, perhaps, if the student learns from the mistakes that were made, then, there can be significant improvement. That is better than the teacher swearing and degrading the individual student. The teacher is thus maintaining the vital respect for a positive learning environment.

In the event there are two or more students involved in a fight in the classroom, action must be taken quickly and decisively. A teacher needs to call the administration immediately. Before the administration arrives, there could be an instance in which a teacher needs to loudly express and demand that the involved students separate themselves to different sides of the classroom. Should they refuse, it is imperative to move the other students to the sides of the classroom or even outside the classroom for their protection and safety. Then, calling the administration again needs to be done quickly.

Due to the fact that we as teachers all remember too well the disruptive students, we could almost expect them to misbehave. Then, they will perceive this from us, and they will fulfill our wish. However, if we were to believe that each day is a new beginning in which all students can behave respectfully and can learn no matter what happened previously, teachers will be showing students that there is not any resentment. In turn, they may not act out, and teachers may have a better learning environment with fewer discipline problems.

Another aspect of respect that needs to be addressed is patience with students. Patience in the classroom is based on a teacher's personality. When impatience is demonstrated to the students, they may feel inferior which may probably create a negative atmosphere. When patience is exhibited, a teacher is showing respect of their humanity.

Nobody is perfect. Students can learn. They can be successful. They also can make mistakes. By making mistakes, whether it be in their behavior or in their academic work, mistakes can be overcome, and they can learn from their mistakes so that they will become better human beings and better students. In fact, mistakes are wake-up calls or gifts to promote some sort of change.

Let's say, one class was absolutely horrible today. Then, a usually much better, well-behaved class is coming in next. What needs to be remembered is that the new class deserves positive attention without the teacher still having a bad mindset due to the previous class. After all, it is not fair to the new class. In fact, having a better class next can most certainly create a better mindset for you, thus restoring your enthusiasm.

With any stored frustration, it is better to deal with it in healthy ways during a preparation period or after school. A teacher could complain to other teachers, walk, run, kickbox, or shout in a secluded area. Whatever approach is used in order to vent frustrations, innocent students should not be the brunt end of a teacher's frustration. All students deserve to learn the knowledge that is shared with them, and they do not need anger. They need an education, guidance, patience, and respect.

The residual effect of being calm and assertive with all students can be very important in your students' lives. You can be their role model, even though they may have given you the most discipline problems. By you acting objectively and with respect of individual differences, you are showing them how to work with people in their personal lives and in their professional lives in the future.

Respect is a two-way street. When respect is demonstrated, respect will be the consequence and reciprocated. Practicing respect in a genuine fashion will enhance their self-respect and their respect of others ultimately.

CHAPTER FOURTEEN

~

The Teacher's Sensitivity of Students

While a teacher is hired to teach a subject to the best of his or her ability, being sensitive of one's students in many ways can be extremely beneficial and is being respectful.

A teacher needs to organize the classroom so it looks appealing for the students to respect, so it is a good idea to see if there are any funds available to buy any kinds of posters related to the subject or subjects being taught and also related to self-esteem and then to place them on the walls. In many respects, how the classroom looks is a reflection of a teacher. Thus, students will be sensitive to how the classroom is organized. When there are posters that reflect the teacher's sensitivity to students, their self-esteem, and the subjects being taught, the classroom is a showcase of respect, sensitivity, and learning.

A teacher needs to be sensitive to each student while still taking care of all students. There may be too many students in an overcrowded classroom with perhaps not even enough chairs at the beginning of the school year. There may be students who do not get along well with one another, those students who have ADD or ADHD who may or may not have taken their medications to calm themselves down, those students with special needs, and those students who may understand English limitedly or not at all. You may be teaching an English as a Second Language class with a multitude of languages presented.

There will be interruptions during classes requiring some students to leave, thus interfering with their education. Hopefully, those students will have written down enough notes to complete their homework for the next school day.

It is impossible to try to be aware of each student's behavior each minute in all of the classes. Since a teacher only has one set of eyes and ears, hopefully there will be fewer instances of student distractions so that teaching can take place.

A teacher also has a very demanding schedule to try to fulfill the educational goals to the best of his or her ability while hoping that the students will understand well enough in order to complete their homework and in order to pass all of their graded assignments.

Considering all of the above, teaching truly can become a huge challenge. It can be looked upon as too enormous of a task.

So how does a teacher retain sensitivity to his or her students along with trying to educate them the best way possible? By giving individual attention, a teacher can make individual progress one student at a time. The rest of this chapter is devoted to enhancing sensitivity without resorting to insensitivity to everyone and without becoming overwhelmed by the magnitude of the student variables of personalities and learning abilities.

If there is access to a phone in your classroom or an e-mail address where you can be reached, please regularly check to find out whether there might be any messages not only during the school day but also during nonschool days. Oftentimes, parents or guardians can leave voice mail messages or e-mails. When it is humanly possible, it is advisable to respond by calling or e-mailing them as soon as possible so that the lines of communication are open between all concerned in order to deal with whatever issues may be involved. In turn, the parents or guardians will truly appreciate your efforts.

There are those unfortunate times when people have accidents or when they have some sort of illness that is life-threatening. This can obviously affect one's emotional stability, and education can thus be the last priority on anyone's mind. Under these circumstances, if a teacher finds out about how a student is affected emotionally by this trauma of a friend or a relative, it is best to allow him or her to go to the counselor in order to discuss the situation. This action focuses on the fact that the student is an emotional human being who needs comfort rather than an education at that moment.

There are those unfortunate times when deaths occur among young adults' families, family friends, or people in the school community. When students are grieving, they may feel obligated to attend class but truly do not feel like being there. If it is apparent that they are showing signs of sadness, it is best to allow them to be escorted by other students or campus monitors to their counselor. In this way, the teacher is respecting their right to grieve while the rest of the class can continue learning.

If the entire class is affected by the death of a very popular student, a popular teacher or administrator, or a community member, the best thing to do under the circumstances is to allow them to talk with each other or else discuss it as an entire class or in small groups. The teacher too may be affected emotionally due to the popularity of this individual. By allowing this grieving process to take place, the teacher is showing the students that he or she respects their right to grieve, and they will be more willing to resume learning again the next school day.

If the entire school has been affected by the death of an individual, there may be additional counselors available to deal with the situation accordingly. It can be very devastating, and even though the education of our youth is important, this is the appropriate time to take care of the emotional healing that needs to take place for all concerned. Afterward, everyone's concentration level and their ability to refocus on learning can be regained.

For the sake of all students' physical, mental, and emotional health, it is essential to be informed about drugs and alcohol. It is a good idea to attend informational meetings or workshops in order to become acquainted with eating disorder problems that afflict our teenage girls especially. Lastly, it is a good idea to attend any informational meetings or workshops oftentimes presented by local police departments to learn about gang-related activities in the school's community. By becoming aware of such societal issues facing our youth, teachers can be on the lookout for any overt or covert problems.

There are all kinds of students in different kinds of living environments. Both parents or guardians typically may have to work. They may have to leave very early and arrive home late, thus allowing some immature kids to rule the home. Of course, they might need to do some chores and homework in order to occupy their time. There are welfare families. There are students who live with only one parent or guardian, students who live with family members other than their parents or guardians, and students who may be living with friends of theirs or in group homes.

There are students who may have been so traumatized by family conditions, family issues, and their peers, that it is difficult for them to focus on anything, let alone on a teacher's lesson plan and the subject being presented. There are students who have become so unruly that their parents or guardians have thrown their own children out of their home and they live with other relatives or with friends. There are students who live out on the streets, and their only refuge is when they attend school to eat meals, to socialize, and to learn.

While there are comically distracting students that can generate minor problems, the students who are very passive or very shy are the ones that can be of great concern. Teachers may try to encourage them to share their viewpoints, but it may be too much of a challenge for them for various reasons. If they lash out in anger in the classroom or if a student is usually very passive and is acting out very aggressively for an extended period of time, there may be a problem being presented, and a teacher needs to be watchful.

They may just lay their heads down on their desks, although they may just be tired possibly from working too much. They may just lay their heads down because they are so sad and are really crying for whatever reason. They may feel so tense that they may be seated in a fetal position.

If a student is usually very outspoken in the classroom and dramatically shifts to being very reserved for an extended period of time, there may be a problem. There definitely could be a multitude of possible problems.

So what does a teacher do to act on behalf of the student in order to resolve an apparent emotional problem?

If there is a major issue being presented sometime during a class period, it is a good idea to write a hall pass and to send this student with another student or a campus monitor to his or her counselor to further investigate the situation.

At the end of class, a teacher may want to ask him or her to stay in the classroom in order to talk for a minute or two to express concern. If he or she seems credible and if the teacher believes there is nothing to be concerned about, the student will know that the teacher is a sensitive, caring teacher and is concerned. If the answer is not credible, it is important to notify his or her counselor as soon as possible so that the counselor can discuss the situation in more detail with the student in question.

Here are some examples for consideration. One student is never a discipline problem, but it is readily apparent that she has some emotional problems. She begins to sob in class. Under the circumstances, she probably needs to see her counselor immediately escorted by another student or a campus monitor.

If a student is showing signs of being depressed in class, the teacher may want to suggest the possibility of being available, if the student wishes to discuss the issue.

No matter what the circumstances are, whether they are major or minor, students need to be recognized as human emotional beings and to be validated. In other words, teachers need to be oftentimes a support system for their students.

Boys too can be very emotional. Here is an example. There is a boy in the class whose home life is not the best because his parents are arguing so very much, which ultimately leads to a divorce. He is an average student. He is comforted by the validation and confidence that is brought to him by the teacher who notices his depression. It is a way to confirm what is apparent. Under the circumstances, he may wish to divulge privately to you more details.

When and if a male student becomes extremely demanding and very angry, being calm while not being argumentative with him may be able to alleviate some of his hostility. He is trying to create some sort of confrontation with someone, and the teacher may be seen as a possible target. By not giving in to this conflict, the teacher can realize that the student has the problem. If it becomes such a disruption in class for the rest of the students, calling the administration and/or a campus monitor as quickly as possible is the best possible way to restore some order.

If this student hopefully chooses to calm down so that learning may be continued, the teacher may want to consider discussing this situation with him at the end of class when the rest of the students have left. If neither one has time then due to their next classes, it is best to suggest talking with him outside the school day in order to discuss this outburst. Should that not be considered an option, it would be best to discuss the situation with his counselor as soon as possible. In turn, the counselor can send for him to delve into the issue.

When and if there are signs of major bruising on the student, it is important to privately discuss with him or her as to how the bruises may have happened. If he or she sounds credible, fine; however, if it is sensed that he or she is covering up the truth, it is a teacher's legal responsibility to notify his or her counselor that day so that the counselor can pursue the situation with the student in more detail. If the counselor believes that more legal action is necessary, he or she will call the appropriate Children Protective Service agency.

It is extremely important to understand that a teacher is dealing with a human being who deserves the right to be treated with dignity and with respect all the time. When and if there are signs of abuse of any form, the student's health needs to be addressed with sensitivity and promptly.

While a teacher may have doubts about notifying his or her counselor, this student's development needs always to be protected without any danger and without any harm whatsoever from anybody. By law, the teacher is protected.

When and if the student is talking to someone inside or outside the classroom and it is overheard that he or she is discussing sexual activity that might have taken place between him or her with an adult or perhaps inappropriate touching by an adult, then it is a teacher's legal responsibility to notify his or her counselor that day so that the matter can be dealt with accordingly and quickly.

When and if there are times in which there may be a student coming to class before school, during the lunch break, and/or after school, it is important to be aware of the fact that the classroom door needs to remain open so that anyone who passes by can see the student and the teacher. Indeed, the student might have a question in regard to the subject that needs to be addressed, and that is perfectly fine.

The problem is when the door is closed, even if there is a window in the door and even if there are clear windows that look into the classroom. It could be perfectly innocent to have the door closed, but should there be an issue that a student has with the teacher, the student can easily make accusations stating some inappropriate behavior took place. In turn, it will be the student's word against the teacher's, and that is not a very good situation for the teacher.

The teacher's reputation can be negatively affected. The teacher can be placed on suspension, fired, or be involved with the police. Even if the teacher is cleared of all allegations, there will always be some suspicion and some distrust remaining by some people with whom he or she associates.

Thus, it is recommended that the classroom door is always open when the teacher is alone in the classroom and will permit students to enter. If it so happens the teacher has the door closed and a student enters, it is best to open the door and to leave the door open.

If the teacher prefers to have some privacy in the classroom in order to take care of some professional tasks or to make some phone calls, it is advisable to shut and lock the door. If a student knocks at the door, the teacher has a choice as to what to do next, either to allow the student to enter with the door open or to suggest another time to discuss whatever needs to be addressed, unless there is an emergency involved.

The above situations do occur, but a teacher's normal day will not be traumatic and eventful in terms of emotional issues. These types of situations can occur, but instruction can take place with minor discipline problems. Sensitivity needs to be keen, but not so overburdening.

A teacher being sensitive to the students' needs will enhance their own sensitivity about themselves and for others. The teacher is thus enhancing mutual respect. Students might even consider becoming teachers, counselors, psychologists, psychiatrists, or social workers, for example, because the teacher has taken the initiative to help them become educated, but also to treat them with the sensitivity and care that they truly deserve.

CHAPTER FIFTEEN

~

Appreciating and Working with Uniqueness

You learned early on how unique you truly were and are. You saw your parents or guardians daily realizing what kinds of people they were, and you determined what qualities they had that you could emulate and which characteristics were not so appealing. You thus developed your own personality with your own likes and dislikes for people and things.

Of course, there might have been times in which you had disagreements with them; however, your similarities and your respect for each other's differences could have been far more prevalent and withstood disagreements for the most part.

As you grew older, you became cognizant of how important it is to work daily with others with whom you agree and with those who were not of your own persuasion while still maintaining respect.

It has been said that "variety is the spice of life." Indeed, there is a lot of variety in life, and that certainly creates that much more diversity in terms of many aspects of our lives. There are people of different body sizes, different personalities, different tolerances, different religions, different cultures, different philosophies, different sexual orientations, different clothing styles, and different makeup styles. Indeed, our world is a major blend of different cultures along with unique people all with their own likes and dislikes.

Let's take a specific example. A student enters your class wearing all black clothing. She wears black makeup on her face except for a black cross with a red cross in the middle of her right cheek. She seems very quiet and does not talk with any of her classmates. As a matter of fact, they ignore her.

One might come up with some very interesting conclusions. She seems to either crave attention or wishes not to be part of the "in" group that wears "standard" high school clothing. She does not want to associate with others because she considers them "weird," and the others in the class also consider her "weird." She might have strange friends with whom she associates.

Your first impression might be that she does not conform to your standards of dressing and makeup, and you might personally believe that she might become a discipline problem.

So what do you do? How do you work with gothic style students along with the normally dressed students? How can you change everyone's perspective so that everyone is engaged in your subject matter?

No matter how students look on the outside, they all deserve an education. You and all of your students are a classroom community for a certain time period, which necessitates cooperation.

To "break the ice" in this regard, please learn to look beyond the exterior in order to find out what the interior is like for all of your students. With time and patience, the classroom community will learn to get along with one another.

The above example of a girl with these gothic tendencies was one of my students. It turns out that she was one of the smartest students in the class. Eventually, the other students learned to respect and appreciate her, and she was able to bond with them.

There are people who are unfortunately resistant to uniqueness or change due to their own biases or sheltered belief systems, and they wish to be exclusive and wish to disregard or avoid others. We have had racial strife. We have had hatred toward different world cultures, colors, religions, belief systems, and gender orientations.

A book and a movie entitled *Black Like Me* was about John H. Griffin, a white man who stayed for a while in the southern United States in 1959. He then painted his face black and went to the same areas and experienced prejudice. Of course, that was a long time ago, and times have changed; however, there are still all kinds of prejudices. What is ironic is that many of these same minorities have been downtrodden themselves and yet they discriminate just as much.

As a result of these prejudices, many schools have implemented different methods of trying to encourage students to get along better with one another. Schools have multicultural assemblies whereby there are different performances of different cultures so that the general student body will have some exposure to people that are different from themselves.

There are organizations that frequent high schools that blend people of different features so that they can discuss in small groups what it means to be who they are and how they are. With such dialogues, these students can relate much better to one another, thus beginning to break down preconceived notions and alleviating a lot of tension between people.

The Southern Poverty Law Center sponsors www.tolerance.org, which includes classroom activities promoting uniqueness, acceptance, and the desire to have equality for everyone.

We all have many similar needs and concerns along with our unique inclinations. We all deserve to recognize and to appreciate one another. By teachers showing students ideas and by their actions, students become more sensitive to others with less criticism and with less derogatory remarks. More acceptance of the uniqueness of others will be the result, even though there may still be differences of opinions.

Whatever is taught, students need variety and diversity in their method to be informed. It does not mean to stand on one's head for them or to perform a circus act. Yet, in order to maintain their interest, they need unique experiences that will make lasting impressions on them. Since students learn in different ways, many different creative approaches need to be considered.

One method that a social studies teacher utilized was to wear a uniform of old American history with a fake rifle in his classroom. Then he would act the part of that person. That certainly drew the attention of his students, and they learned a lot from this experience.

A business teacher at our high school developed a student store, and the students now complete all the normal operations of a regular business at school during school time with the appropriate teacher supervision.

An art teacher and his students have painted major artists' masterpieces on the barren walls of our campus. This has allowed these artistic students to learn how to appreciate art and the history and the intent of the original painters. Also, the rest of the student body is proud of each other's work and has that much more pride in their school.

One way to inspire creative and critical thinking skills in students is to ask them open-ended questions. *The Kids' Book of Questions* by Gregory Stock can help to inspire diverse thinking with hypothetical questions that have no right or wrong answers. There might be questions that fit your subject area. Also, this book of questions could be a great tool toward the end of a class session when the teacher would not want to introduce anything else. Then general questions could be asked from this book in order to find out how students think about different issues. In this way, students learn how to think more critically and listen to their fellow classmates. Incidentally, Gregory Stock has written a more adult version entitled *The Book of Questions* that could also be used, based on the maturity of your students and your subjects.

There are those students who are naturally shy and just simply want to blend in, in order to not stand out in the crowd. Group work can open a whole new realm of possibilities for these students to gain self-confidence and self-worth so that they feel more comfortable with themselves and with others. Nevertheless, it will take time and maturity for them to get out of their emotional shell. Also, when relatively vocal students work with naturally shy students, both types of personalities can gain a better appreciation of one another.

Besides the shy students, there are students who wish to always be the center of attention without regarding the rights of others. For instance, they may always have their hand up in order to respond to a teacher's questions, or they may try to shout out their answers so that the whole class will hear them. The best way to handle this situation is to tactfully suggest that other points of view need to be heard. Afterward, please ask other students to share their points of view. In this way, the more outspoken students may become more sensitive of others.

By validating uniqueness, you teach students to reduce their prejudices and look at individuals for who they are instead of what they look like and/or what their backgrounds consist of. By teaching with critical thinking activities, you teach students to become better thinkers. By teaching with creativity, you keep students from becoming bored.

An interesting side benefit of listening to student viewpoints is that teachers can become that much more informed about how students view the world, that much more inspired, and that much more excited about teaching and learning, no matter what kind of academic class and no matter what kind of students are being taught. In turn, discipline problems may become minimal, and there is that much more mutual respect.

CHAPTER SIXTEEN

~

Consistent Fairness

It is highly important for the teacher to be comfortable with the classroom rules that are formulated. When there are misbehaviors, the teacher needs to easily adhere to the designed rules. If not, revising the rules is critical so that students will perceive the rules as a reflection of his or her personality, thus enforcing fairness for all concerned.

Here is something to consider. If you were a student in your own class, could you abide by your own rules? Would these rules be considered fair? Would other students consider them fair?

Here are some possible suggestions for consideration. When being hired to become a teacher in a district, a contract needs to be signed. There are certain standards or expectations to follow. With that in mind, how about considering a student contract? The contract can consist of their rights to learn the subject matter and to be respected as individuals. After an explanation of their rights, the student contract can specify their responsibilities as to what is expected of them both inside the classroom (appropriate behavior, paying attention, and taking class notes, for example) and outside the classroom (how much time to study and to do homework, for example) to be successful.

It can include the consequences of inappropriate behavior in the classroom: detention, phone call to the parents, student-parent-teacher-administrator meetings, suspensions, and even possibly expulsions, for example. It also can include the consequences of choosing not to do homework: little or no learning and poor grades, for example.

After developing such a student contract, you can distribute, read, and discuss this student contract in class and answer any questions they may have during the first day or two of the school year. Then it is advisable for them to take it home to read by themselves and to have the parents or guardians read and sign it as well. This can be a homework assignment that can be required for your records.

Instead of the student contract idea, a lot of teachers just simply have four or five rules that are posted on their bulletin boards and are discussed with the class at the beginning of the school year. Here is one possible example of student behavior and expectations that can be posted:

1. Students will arrive on time for class.
2. Students will be respectful of other students and of the teacher.
3. Students need paper, pens, and pencils for this class to take notes.
4. Students are not to use their cell phones in any way during class.
5. Students will study assigned readings, will complete written home-work, and will complete the graded assignments, like quizzes and tests, to the best of their ability.

Some teachers prefer not to come up with the discipline rules themselves. They ask the students to determine which rules they themselves can live by. Once those rules are determined, the teachers may want to discuss or suggest methods of how the behavior and discipline procedures can be improved, if at all. Invariably, most students will devise rules that are the same or even more stringent than what the teachers suggest. Bottom line, the reason for dealing with classroom management in this fashion is so that most students will more than likely comply with these kinds of rules more readily.

Of course, however the rules are established for the classroom, teachers also need to adhere to school policies. For example, most high schools have a general tardy policy that is important to understand and to comply with:

1. If the students have one tardy, does the teacher need to assign deten-tion?
2. If they have more than one tardy, what are the school's policies?

Upon creating classroom procedures for students or with students, there needs to be consistent impartiality. Teachers are paid to teach their subject so that everyone is always treated fairly. Under these circumstances, trust and respect for their teachers will be the end result. There will also be a more positive classroom environment with fewer discipline problems.

Nevertheless, if there is favoritism to any degree for any student or students, it will eventually result in distrust and lack of respect for their teachers. Like a bad apple in a bag of good apples, favoritism will result in students understanding the situation very well and usually will react negatively or will try to get on the "favorites' list" so that they can easily receive attention and better grades. The classes will become contaminated with a lot of negativity and ill feelings by the students, and it will be difficult to restore order.

There can be student-parent-teacher-administrator meetings in order to resolve the issue at hand. It can become a very nasty situation, and there will be a total disregard of the teachers involved. Even if the teachers admit favoritism was practiced and even if the teachers decide to practice consistent impartiality with everybody, the students will look for any signs of favoritism afterward, only to use any slight form of partiality against the teachers, resulting possibly in more discipline issues and more meetings.

Also, in the long term, students have a great memory. Even if they do not have those particular teachers the following school year, they can and will tell other students who will have those teachers as to how favoritism is practiced. Indeed, it can be an uphill battle that will be extremely difficult to overcome.

When it comes to practicing impartiality in terms of quizzes and tests in which there is only one answer, it is either right or wrong, and the appropriate evaluation can take place. If it is totally wrong, then points are deducted. If it is partially right and partially wrong (for example: it is a two-part question in which the student has one part correct and one part incorrect), it is easy to determine partial credit. Upon grading the entire quiz or test, you can just add up the points and determine the final grade based on the percentages you, the department, and the high school have determined.

When it comes to short answers and essay assignments, a consistent method of evaluating what the students are stating needs to be determined, including what needs to be given appropriate points and what needs to be deducted for errors. If there are department-wide evaluation methods, it is important to be consistent and to adhere by the same standards since if students do take subsequent classes in the department, they will understand the department's expectations.

If there are no department-wide standards when it comes to short answers and essay assignments, it is desirable to devise one's own methods and to discuss this possible procedure with department teachers prior to school starting. If these ideas are approved by the department, fine. Upon approval and if they do work, students will benefit accordingly. Upon approval by the department and if they do not work, more research needs to be done with staff members for a better evaluation method.

It is important to update points or grades ideally on a daily basis, whether it is by using a computer program and/or documenting them only in the grade book. It may take a couple of extra minutes each day to do this for each class, but it is certainly worth it.

Think of it in this way. When there is a request to determine a student's points or grade, you can easily access that information with a minimum amount of work. If the points or grades are not updated, you may have to record data, thus delaying the requested grade. Also, when grades are due to the administration for progress reports, quarter grades, and semester grades, it becomes much easier to determine grades when all the data are updated.

There is one aspect of grades that needs to be addressed, and that is the emotional side of grades. While you have designed a grading system that can be utilized for the most amount of fairness, most students will truly know and will truly accept the grade that they have earned. For example, when the points are tabulated at the end of a grading period, there is not a need for any confrontation when there is the appropriate documentation to support their final grades. Of course, if there are errors, it is essential for trust and respect to correct any errors in question.

If any students become rather irate and demanding that their grade is unfairly given, it is best to be as calm as possible. Then you need to ask the students to discuss the situation civilly so that there can be a better atmosphere in which the problem can be resolved with mutual respect intact.

If the students finally agree that the grade is correct but do not like the grade, they can realize that they need to study more and to do their best in all of their work. They will also learn more about responsibility to determine their own grades. After all, a teacher is like a mirror, only reflecting what students have been accomplishing and what has not been accomplished successfully.

If the students would not agree with the final grade, it would be advantageous to tabulate the specific grades and points for the entire grading period with them present. If, in fact, students are correct and there is a need to adjust the grade, please do so since this would be the fair thing to do.

Students who earn consistently average, below average, and poor grades can be the more challenging ones. You may believe you have let them down since they have not learned well enough or improved their grades. While this might prompt feeling bad, it is important to realize that teachers can only teach, encourage, and inspire students so much. Students are responsible for what they do inside and outside the classroom. They have to take the initiative for taking responsibility for their own actions. They need to become self-accountable, self-actualizing individuals to learn and to ask questions about the material that they might not understand.

If you can motivate underachieving students so that their learning and their grades are increased, congratulations for your work with them, and please continue encouraging and praising them.

What needs to be discussed is when a majority of the students might do exceedingly poor work on a graded assignment, like on a quiz or on a test. You thus need to examine the entire scenario:

1. In retrospect, where could you have presented the information more clearly so that more students could understand it better?
2. Did your students have enough time with this information?
3. Did your students have enough practice with this information?
4. Were your students paying enough attention, or were they being disruptive?

Under these circumstances, it may mean utilizing different methods of learning the information, such as more visual projects and/or computer software programs dealing with this subject matter. Perhaps fellow teachers in the department can help with their suggestions.

As for the grade that they had earned for the semester, please consider one of several options. The first quarter grade and the second quarter grade could count equally, or you could count the higher of the two grades. If the grade would be lower for the second quarter, the second quarter grade would be reflective as to what progress has been made or lack thereof. If the grade would be higher for the second quarter, the second grade would count. It all depends on what you believe is a fair option based on the circumstances. The rest of the semester would be determined by the final exam, if final exams are given at your high school.

There are schools that not only have an academic grade, but they also include a citizenship grade. If your high school has a method of determining citizenship grades, please adhere to their procedure for the sake of fairness for all the students.

If there is not a set procedure for assessing citizenship at your high school, please devise a way to assess citizenship that is appropriate and comfortable for you and so that your students are fully aware of your evaluation of their citizenship. You could devise a point system in which the students start with one hundred points. You could determine which bad behaviors would deduct points. It would be a good idea to have a piece of paper on which you document the students' names, the dates of the behaviors, and specific behaviors that are inappropriate.

Oftentimes, both academic grades and citizenship grades are important as to whether or not students will be able to be involved in school activities for a certain portion of time. It is a great way to have the students become more self-accountable and more cooperative.

When teachers discuss their contracts or their rules with their students at the beginning of the school year, students learn that there are certain expectations of them to be known and to be followed. These expectations need to be realistic so that the classroom can function in a smooth fashion in which everyone will have an equal opportunity to succeed when they apply themselves.

When teachers practice fairness with all students, teachers are modeling what it means to be living in the adult world. They become that much more mature in their thinking, and they become that much more sensitive of others' expectations.

CHAPTER SEVENTEEN

~

The Challenging Students

Unmotivated students can come from life experiences resulting in them being unwilling to learn, angry, and/or dejected. Oftentimes, these unmotivated students only seek the negative because they feel unworthy of anything positive, resulting in many of these students simply not being inspired unfortunately, no matter what kinds of positive comments are made. So teachers can have a big challenge to try to motivate challenging students.

They may need counseling to surpass their issues. It may be very tempting to say that they need counseling directly to them; however, that expressed opinion may come across as being too harsh. After all, the teachers' primary reason for being in the classroom is to teach, and parents or guardians would probably be outraged.

Under these circumstances, it is important to discuss these students with their counselors with specific observations noted. Then the counselors can take the initiative to assist these students.

The other possibility would be if the teachers were able to have a good relationship with the students in question. The students might reveal their concerns, and the teachers might be able to give some friendly, tactful advice on how to handle their situations or to refer them to their high school counselor.

Another possibility for your consideration is to organize a meeting of all of the student's teachers and the counselor in order to discuss him or her. Each teacher could discuss his or her perspective as to what has worked and what has not worked. If a remedy is found by such a meeting, perhaps the rest of the teachers can use this technique to inspire him or her. If nothing seems to have worked, it is important for the counselor to talk with him or her about school, learning, and life at home, for example.

When it comes to educational issues, the unmotivated students can be reached by focusing attention on what they might not understand, by sitting down at their level, by talking *with* them and *not to* them, which can help build their self-confidence. The distinction between talking *with* and *not to* is very important because students oftentimes are told what to do without anyone listening to them. As a matter of fact, when teachers become frustrated and angry and resort to talking *to* them, students may actually disregard what is being said, even though they know what is being said is the truth and can be helpful.

An example of a dialogue that could lead to students achieving more success could be the following:

> *The teacher:* How's this class going for you lately?
> *The student:* I don't know.
> *The teacher:* What has been easy for you?
> *The student:* What we did at the beginning of the school year was very easy.
> *The teacher:* And what about lately?
> *The student:* I don't know.
> *The teacher:* You seem to be struggling with this information nowadays. Is that correct?
> *The student:* Yeah, I guess.
> *The teacher:* What can I do to help you so that you can feel more comfortable with this information?
> *The student:* Well, when you explained about . . .

Suffice it to say that this will not happen in every single instance and immediately; however, when students are given more individual attention by teachers who listen to them and ask open-ended questions, learning can improve, and students' confidence in themselves can be a side benefit.

Here is another unmotivated student with low self-esteem. She is barely a C-average student, but it seems to be apparent that she wants to improve. All she might need is patience, respect, encouragement, tact, and attention. While it may be embarrassing for her, she truly wants and appreciates the individual attention by the teacher.

With the proper encouragement by the teacher, she can improve her self-confidence and her ability to understand the information of the class. It may take a short period of time or a long period of time. She may come to realize that she too is an important member of the class wanting to learn the information better.

All you can do is to encourage and guide to the best of your ability while being respectful of students' personalities and abilities. It needs to be remembered that even if students have not shown great improvement, it does not mean that will continue and remain so-called underachievers. You are like a light switch that can illuminate students personally and academically. If you are successful, you are to be congratulated for your efforts. If you have a minimum amount of success, you are making some minute headway to changing behaviors. If they are not receptive, at least the effort was made, and that is what counts.

All students need is the teachers' persistent, fair, sincere manner of helping. Then students need to make a choice to want to change for the better. If they do so, the teachers may see a dramatic shift in their attitude, in their behavior, and in their studies in all of their classes.

Who knows? One teacher, maybe you, could be the driving force for them to want to change their lives now so that their future will be more positive.

There is a website that you may want to explore, www.goodcharacter.com, which contains many interesting activities to utilize with all students for self-worthiness and to increase self-responsibility.

Ultimately, challenging students subconsciously wish to be reached, to feel good about themselves, and to have a better life. Teachers can help them by what they say and by what they do on a regular basis. For those students who wish not to be challenged academically but wish to be challenging in terms of their behavior, all that can be done is to work with them individually as much as possible. Hopefully, they will change their perspective. They need "to step up to the plate" to want to cooperate and to learn.

CHAPTER EIGHTEEN

~

Tech-Savvy Students

Life can be complicated. We have so many distractions that occupy our mind at home, at work, and outside when not at work.

At home, we can be distracted by our landline phones, our cell phones, our televisions, our DVD players, our radios, our CD players, our computers, and even our family members, even though we need and love our family members to balance our lives. The technological devices are controlled by the individuals who own them, but it seems that there are a lot of people who are almost obsessed to the degree that it is almost replacing one-on-one interactions with people.

At work, we have professional responsibilities requiring us oftentimes to utilize landline phones, televisions, DVD players, CD players, and computers. Technology in the school environment has become increasingly important to keep up with the outside world and our global economy.

Even when we are not at home or at work, we can involve ourselves with distractions with our cell phones and GPS devices, for example. While cell phones are helpful to be in communication with people, they truly can become dangerous, especially when people wish to dial and text while driving at the same time. If people utilize GPS devices, it is vital to not be driving and pressing them where to go. A voice-operating GPS device is much better and safer.

Yes, we truly have become reliant upon technology. In a sense, we have become slaves of our own technological devices because there are so many of us who become dependent and wonder how we could have lived prior to them. Just think of Hal, the sensitive computer in the movie *2001: A Space Odyssey*. Our students are truly reliant on technology.

So how should a teacher handle tech-savvy students who continually wish to distract themselves even in the classroom? Granted, there is a time and a place for technology in the classroom. When they are supposed to be doing projects and Internet searches, computers can then be very helpful. Of course, by monitoring what they are doing on the computers, teachers can determine how well focused they are because while most of them will be cooperative, there will invariably be those students who will try to look at websites that are inappropriate for them or try to play computer games instead.

Besides computers, an even more challenging distraction that teachers encounter is cell phones and texting. Since cell phones include so many other applications other than phone calling, students seem to be obsessed with them for their communication via texting, their games, taking pictures, and so on.

Indeed, if students believe they will not be caught, they can be texting messages underneath their desks to others in the same classroom, in the next classroom, in another part of the school, or off campus entirely. It could be to communicate teenage messages or to share answers in regard to quizzes and tests.

Since the temptation is so strong to be texting, classroom rules about cell phone usage of any kind need to be coordinated with the school rules. It is important to require the students' full attention to their teachers, meaning they should turn off their cell phones, if that is in accordance with school policy. Another option can be that the cell phones can be on silent mode and not even the vibration mode so that they will not be a distraction during class whatsoever. If this is how teachers will allow cell phones, it is very important to emphasize that students are not to be checking their cell phones during any time of class due to the need and the benefit of their learning, which requires their full attention.

In the event that there are students who have forgotten or who are being defiant regarding turning off their cell phones, it is best to enforce your rules or the school's rules right away so that there will be less likelihood of any more problems in the future by any of the students.

An example of enforcement could be to inform students at the very beginning of the school year that cell phone usage is not tolerated whatsoever. The first time of defiance could be a warning. The second time of defiance could be to take their cell phone away until the end of the class period. The third time of defiance could be to take their cell phone away and for them to pick it up after school. The fourth time of defiance could be to have a parent-student-teacher conference about this issue. The fifth time of defiance could be to refer the students to their dean.

Should students become defiant regarding the rules that are established for the classroom, perhaps it would be best to refer them to the administration immediately.

Since students have so many distractions in their home while they are trying to complete their homework, it is best to suggest at the beginning of the school year and to oftentimes remind them during the school year that they will accomplish a lot more work efficiently and in less time when they focus entirely on their homework. You could ask them if they wish to complete all of their homework in a short period of time or in a long period of time. More than likely, they wish it to be as short as possible. In turn, you could suggest that they turn off their technological devices. It will be their choice and their responsibility as to how long and how thoroughly they complete their homework.

Although it may be a little bit costly, please consider buying a separate cell phone specifically for communication with students and parents or guardians. It can thus be a tax write-off as well. It is best to have a professional cell phone number if you wish to be contacted and if you wish to have contact with your students. If not, your opinion is to be respected.

There are many teachers who utilize cell phone texting with their students to their advantage. Teachers have sent text messages to their students to assign homework, quizzes, and tests when the students have been absent or as reminders to all students present in class that day. Students can send text messages to their teachers relating to the information that they have covered, or they may want to find out about future assignments, quizzes, and tests.

There is an interesting ramification for today's youth due to our oftentimes swift technological advances. While they know that learning information and earning decent grades will require work on their part, they wish to have everything done instantaneously. When the information is easy for them, fine. When it becomes a challenge or overpowering for them, they will show their resistance or make up excuses for not learning the information.

Thus, students need to be reminded that it takes regular work, time, and patience in order to achieve any degree of mastery of the subject matter. They will then learn that the quality of their work will result in whatever grade they justly earn. They will also then learn how to dedicate themselves that much more so, if they choose to put the effort into their work. It can also be a wake-up call for them to seek extra help from their teachers and/or their peers.

An interesting way to utilize current technology is in the following manner. Provided that students utilize a computer with a webcam, they can download programs like Skype (www.skype.com) in order to see one another and talk with one another via their computers. This can be an ideal way for them to communicate and to study.

Indeed, technology can be helpful in the school community, provided that students use it efficiently for their education.

CHAPTER NINETEEN

~

Students Need
and Respect Organization

Which teacher in your past is memorable as being very well organized? Was this helpful for you? More than likely, his or her organization was very helpful because you could learn the information better in a logical sequence.

In order to be very successful in class with students, the teacher's organizational skills are an essential ingredient. He or she needs to consider if there will be full class periods to teach each day of the week or if there will be school activities that will necessitate shortened class periods.

He or she needs to judge how much time to devote to presenting and to practicing new concepts with students as well as student presentations, if desired. He or she needs to determine how much homework is needed for each school night. He or she needs to figure out how much time is required for reviewing homework assignments along with how much time the average student will take for completing quizzes and tests.

It is best for the teacher to determine the workload for all classes. It can be advantageous to design lesson plans to fully complete one's obligations to students without compromising their work, meaning it is worthwhile to balance the load of the work in order to feel less stress and to do a thorough job of evaluating student work. For example, if the teacher has two preparations (for example, Algebra I and Algebra II), it is best to consider having a graded assignment to be completed by Algebra I students one day while maybe having a graded assignment to be completed by Algebra II students another day, if at all possible. It is also advantageous so that the quality of correcting student work will not be jeopardized due to being tired.

Here is something else to consider when it comes to lesson planning. If the teacher begins with chapter 1, then progresses to chapter 5, then digresses to chapter 3 and so forth, students can easily become confused. Students need to see organization in the planning of their learning. Also, the textbook is designed with a specific purpose for each chapter based on the learning and the understanding of the previous chapter.

Having good organizational skills can truly help students learn the information in a logical way. They can conceivably enjoy or at least respect the class that much more, which will hopefully and ultimately translate into fewer discipline problems because they will feel less frustrated about the presentation of the material.

Besides determining the lesson plans for the week, it can be helpful to write down the agenda for each day's class on a piece of paper or on a three by five card so that the teacher can refer to it in order to remain on task during the class period. It would also be best to look at one's watch or the clock every once in a while in order to see how much more time is left to complete what needs to be accomplished for the day.

In terms of student essays, the teacher needs to guide the students not only to write down ideas according to their theme but also to prioritize the list of the actual essay being written. The teacher can show them how mapping can be an effective tool to get themselves organized and ready for their writing assignment so that their ideas are in a logical order. Another idea would be to suggest that students open up a Word document on a computer in which they can type their ideas and move them around so that their ideas make sense, if this is permitted.

Since there will be students who need extra help, here are some suggestions, if not known already. First, the teacher should let students know when he or she is available for them before and/or after school. Secondly, the high school may already have implemented a peer studying program that the students may want to utilize. Lastly, there are probably some websites that publishers utilize that can help students with the practice and the comprehension of each chapter or unit.

As for the organization of the school and its curriculum, there are different philosophies involved. Of course, there is the normal format in which students will take the standard curriculum, which is pertinent for what is considered traditional. There are classes for students of below average, average, and above average intelligence. The so-called below average students will take basic classes, which will give a minimum amount of a challenge. The so-called average students will take classes that can be considered more challenging. The so-called above average students are the ones who will take what is normally considered college preparatory, honors, and advanced placement classes.

There are those high schools that specialize in certain subjects, such as vocational and college preparatory classes. In many respects, students attending these high schools have more of a focus as to what they want to do with their lives eventually.

While the above kinds of high schools have their advantages, there should be more high schools that include a lot of articulation and coordination of their programs with feeder schools, such as elementary and middle schools, and there needs to be more communication about articulation and coordination within the high schools themselves. For instance, it would be ideal to have teachers of the departments of art, sciences, mathematics, English, social studies, and even religion, if offered, to discuss how they can still teach their subjects, but in a way in which the students can learn how each of these subjects can be interrelated. In this way, students can see the sequential relevancy of each class for their total learning.

No matter what kind of class the teacher has, organization is a key element for student success. The more he or she can begin with the basic concepts and to evolve to the complex concepts, the better are the chances that students will see the logic of the material when they apply themselves. Even if they do not necessarily understand the material well when it becomes more complex, this is an opportunity for them to relearn the information from the very beginning by means of reviewing notes, quizzes, and tests and asking questions of the teacher in order for them to hopefully understand the subject matter better.

CHAPTER TWENTY

~

That's Neat!

Male teachers need to wear ties particularly at the beginning of the school year so that students understand that the classroom is formal in many respects. Wearing more formal clothes at the beginning of the school year is important for establishing boundaries and expectations.

Should male teachers wear shirts that are not tucked in and sandals, this gives the appearance of more informality, possibly resulting in discipline problems. More than likely, a colleague and/or an administrator would make a comment about this kind of appearance. If after a while, it is permissible and desired to be less formal and more casual, so be it.

Female teachers need to give the demeanor of being in charge in professional-looking attire as well. This means wearing nice outfits with comfortable shoes, but not wearing high heel shoes because there is enough to do to balance a lesson plan, let alone oneself! If, after a while, it is desired to be less formal and more casual, so be it as well.

In essence, it is important for male and female teachers to portray themselves as professionals worthy of respect from the very beginning. At the same time, it is important for teachers to feel comfortable in their attire since this comfort factor can be sensed by students.

Students need to dress appropriately for the school environment. There are probably rules that they must adhere to, and it is important for the teacher to be cognizant of how they are dressed. There usually will not be an issue of improper dress; however, should any student dress inappropriately, he or she should be sent to the administration.

Neatness and cleanliness in the classroom also set the stage for high expectations from the students. By showing them that the desk and other equipment are organized, neat, and clean, it shows how the teacher shows respect for himself or herself, and that respect for the classroom environment and for the teacher is desired.

The teacher's desk should have the following. There should be lined paper available for those students who need paper. There should be a stapler for them to use with enough staples in it. There should be tissues when and if they and the teacher need them. There should be nothing expensive on the teacher's desk because while most students are good and respectful, if there would be a temptation to steal something valuable, someone might want to steal it.

It is helpful to have a functioning pencil sharpener. It would be best to emphasize to the students that they sharpen their pencils before class and not during class since that can lead to everyone being distracted by the students getting out of their desks and the noise of the pencil sharpener itself. It would be a good idea to suggest to them that they have several sharpened pencils and working pens with them at all times. Also, unless the janitorial staff does this, please empty the pencil sharpener every other day.

The seats and/or the tables need to be arranged in some sort of order to accentuate the fact that the classroom setting is for learning and so that the students and the teacher can walk into and through the classroom with ease.

In an art class, neatness is very desirable as much as possible to get access to the materials needed and for safety purposes. The teacher does not want paint spilling onto the floor creating a possible hazard and a mess for people.

In a science class, being neat, clean, and careful is imperative so that nobody will be injured.

In any class that requires writing, it would be ideal for the school to require students to write their name, their class, their class period, and the date on the top of the paper to be turned in. Thus, students know what is expected and desired.

In any class that requires writing, the teacher needs to remind students to write in either black or blue ink or a dark, black pencil, if this is preferred. Students need to write legibly so that their work can be read and understood. If not, the teacher can misunderstand what the overall meaning and implications are for the writing assignment. It is important to mention to students that it is essential to write legibly on a continuous basis because when they work in the "real world," while computers are used frequently, there will be plenty of instances in which writing will be required.

If typed work is preferred, the consistent style and the consistent size need to be related to the students. A side benefit is that it will be less visually straining for the teacher.

While student writing needs to be neat, it is also important that teachers write neatly. In this way, students will be able to understand what is written on the classroom boards and what the responses are when returning assignments, quizzes, and tests. In turn, they will be able to understand and to utilize the information correctly for future assignments, quizzes, and tests.

Along with sequential learning, when a teacher is neat in the classroom in his or her work, the desire for cleanliness by the students may be met better on a consistent basis.

CHAPTER TWENTY-ONE

~

Questioning Can Lead
to Successful Understanding

You initially learned the information that you are now teaching with a lot of time and a lot of practice. There probably were times in which you needed to ask questions. In turn, you received your needed answers. By not asking questions, you might have been able to pick up the information from the textbook or from another student. If not, you would have been lost, not knowing the answers to your questions. Studying and questioning then were important for learning, which enables you to share this information with students now.

The teacher is not in the classroom to show that he or she is the only authority of this subject and that nobody can have the same command of the material. The teacher needs to create an atmosphere in the classroom where the information is shared in a logical fashion, starting off simply with loads of practice and student questions. If a teacher is talking a majority of the class period, learning does not necessarily take place. Learning is not just simply the listening and the practicing of information. It also requires a complete interaction between the teachers and the students. So how does one create an acceptable, questioning atmosphere in the classroom?

Please consider the following ideas as validations of what you are already doing or consider implementing them for your students' sake.

Students need to be able to feel comfortable enough to ask questions. This means that the teacher is receptive to listening to their questions without judgment. After all, they are asking the questions because they simply do not know or they may have forgotten the studied information.

If their questions deal with an area to be covered in the future, it is desirable to answer it then, if it takes a relatively short period of time. If it will take some time to answer a complicated question and/or the answer is based on information that still needs to be learned, it is best to tactfully suggest that this topic is a bit complicated and will be discussed in the near future once they understand some other aspects of the subject matter. Students will thus know that any question related to their class is appropriate, and they will feel assured that their questions are accepted without hostility and/or sarcasm. In this way, that much more mutual respect can be attained.

Another way to have questions answered of previously studied material is for other students to respond. More than likely, there will be someone in the class who knows the answer. If a student answers correctly, great. If a student answers incorrectly, perhaps the teacher can tactfully ask others for their answers. This technique is another way for respect to be maintained, and this approach shows that the teacher values them as intelligent individuals. If nobody is able to answer the question correctly, of course, please answer the question to clarify the information.

Some teachers use the Question Box technique in which students can write down their questions on a piece of paper and put them in the Question Box at the end of class. The teachers open up the box and read the questions at the end of the school day. The teachers then answer those questions at the beginning of the next day's class. This can be a very effective tool for those students who feel too shy or embarrassed to say anything in class in front of his or her peers or for those who feel that others will judge him or her as being "stupid," for example.

Nevertheless, there are students who may be too immature and unwisely write horrible comments instead and turn them in to the Question Box. If teachers decide to implement this idea and if this immature behavior happens several times, it is best not to continue with the Question Box idea. In that eventuality, the classes need to be informed as to what has happened, and if there are any students who have legitimate questions and do not wish to bring up these questions in class, they need to hand over the written questions with their names on the papers turned in directly to the teachers, which can be answered at the beginning of the next day's class.

As was mentioned in an earlier chapter, *The Kids' Book of Questions* by Gregory Stock can be a great resource for students to understand one another better and for the teacher to understand them better. Perhaps the students might ask the teacher for his or her opinion as well.

In many ways, education promotes rote learning. We expect students to learn basic information, which requires memorizing information. While they need to learn the basics of a class, they also should be able to apply this information in discussions and in compositions.

For example, to generate critical and creative thinking, an English teacher might be interested in asking the following questions:

1. How is your life different from five years ago? How do you suppose your life is going to be different five years from now?
2. What do you suppose are some of the main reasons why the author wrote this book or this short story?
3. How do you interpret this character's actions in this story? Are they justifiable? Why or why not? If you would disagree with this character's actions, what would you have done, and why?
4. Which character do you relate to the most in this story, and why?
5. What do you suppose happens after the end of the book? How will the characters change?

In science classes, we expect students to learn specific terminologies. After learning this information, it would be a good idea for students to consider these types of sample questions, if not used already:

1. Why do you suppose learning this information is relevant to you? Why or why not?
2. How can this experiment have any practical purpose in our society today? Give examples.
3. Was this experiment in your science class easy or challenging? Why or why not?
4. Was this experiment important enough to be done in the first place? Why or why not?
5. Can you compare this experiment to any other experiments that you have done in this class so far? What conclusions can you determine?

We need students to think about what they have learned and to question, to "think outside the box" so that their maturing minds will flourish and thus become more critical, creative, and innovative in their thinking. Then they can produce better lives for themselves personally and possibly professionally, if they decide to major in a studied field at a higher institution of learning and to pursue a career in this subject. Even if these thinking exercises are not necessarily appealing to them, they still will have evolved in their ability to have different perspectives and to formulate opinions, no matter which field of study they pursue.

There is an interesting ramification by questioning students. For those students who feel timid, they may open up more and gain more confidence with time. For those students who are rather impatient of others who may not understand the information as quickly, they may learn to become more patient and more understanding. With all students becoming more sensitive to questions and with them being more sensitive to one another, the teacher may have instilled within all students more empathy and more acceptance of one another and of the teacher. Fewer discipline problems may then take place, thus creating a more positive environment where questions of the subject matter can be freely expressed and where answers can be shared.

~

CHAPTER TWENTY-TWO

High Expectations

If we teach the same way each day of each year, the result will be the same. We might be doing a fine job of teaching; however, there could always be room for improvement. For example, we could still be using old typewriters instead of computers and printers, which allow for a lot of possibilities. If we would use rote learning continuously, we would be teaching driver's education with a book instead of a book along with computer games allowing students to simulate driving experiences with the eventual goal of letting students drive behind the wheel of a car.

Granted, there are many great educational methods that have been used in the past and will continue being used because they have been very helpful and successful with students. Yet, while respecting these methods, these methods can be and have been modified, and even more creative ideas can blossom. Our students need to become inspired to learn, and education can be that much more enjoyable for all concerned.

In order to acquire high expectations from students, it is important to understand what they are capable of doing and understanding at any given time, and they need to reach a certain level of competency in the class by the end of the school year. Thus, the teacher and perhaps the department need to design lesson plans accordingly.

By giving students a realistic, achievable challenge, the teacher is helping them to expand their knowledge of the subject matter, and they can truly feel more confident. If and when the students have difficulty with new concepts, the teacher needs to redesign the lesson plans so that they can improve their understanding.

There is a uniquely sensitive organization that can be beneficial, if you do not know about it already, which is called TESA, which stands for Teacher Expectations and Student Achievement. The Los Angeles County Office of Education has workshops that deal with school communities' perceived prejudices so that there are better relationships in the classroom and better learning. Their website is www.streamer3.lacoe.edu/tesa. It is a great workshop that helps anyone to have higher expectations for their students. If you do not live in California, it is best to do a Google search in your state to determine if there is a similar program there.

The remaining portion of this chapter deals with specific ideas for high expectations that have been tried and can be successful with most students. In many respects, these ideas resulted out of necessity due to the fact that certain methods were not working. In other words, "necessity is the mother of invention."

Please choose from the following ideas that suit you the best, and if not, please just know that these ideas do work nonetheless. Also, since you are unique in your own way, if it is believed that modifications are necessary, please do so in order to benefit your students and you.

Idea Number One

When standing for a significant amount of time typically in front of the class, a teacher's body, particularly the back and the feet, can get tired, and he or she may want to sit down. If the teacher sits down behind a desk during class, it is difficult to instruct the class unless there is a PowerPoint presentation, which may mean using a remote control device or going to a computer a lot in order to change the frames.

So if the administration and fellow staff members will approve the idea, please buy a stool for yourself. Indeed, it can be more comfortable and less tiring when being so inclined to sit down. "Comfortable" is the operative word because there can be an atmosphere of less stress and more relaxation for all concerned. The classroom lesson plans can thus be presented in a more relaxing manner.

A stool would also be of benefit when it comes to monitoring students for quizzes and tests along with roaming around the classroom at different times.

Idea Number Two

With so many different obligations to be done during the school day, it is very important to have a way to be reminded of meetings and phone calls, for example. If a teacher already has a technological device like a cell phone with a calendar and time feature, that is fine as long as it is referred to each day. Another way to handle reminders is to place a piece of paper in a convenient place and to refer to it each day. No matter how a teacher is reminded of different obligations, it is important to fulfill them as well as possible.

Idea Number Three

Along with a student contract or having basic rules posted in the classroom as was discussed in an earlier chapter, please consider distributing a student information sheet that could include their name, their address, their home and cell phone numbers, their e-mail address, their reasons for taking the class, any special concerns that they may have, and their birthday.

When they return the student information sheet, it is important to read their noted information in order to be aware of their own uniqueness. Also, please mark somewhere, like in the lesson plan book or on separate pieces of paper, when their birthdays are.

Please consider the following concerning their birthdays. When and if there is a graded assignment, like a quiz, a test, or a major project due, if it is their birthday, please give them extra credit or extra points. Should there not be any graded assignment on their birthday, they would not earn any extra points or extra credit.

If his or her birthday falls on a weekend or during a vacation, please have a separate piece of paper with the numbers one through thirty-one. Then please write his or her name next to the number of the birthday.

For example, let's say a student has a birthday on July 30, and there is no school in session. Since this is the case and since the student cannot possibly earn extra credit or extra points, for example, should there be a graded assignment on January 30, he or she would earn extra points or extra credit at that time.

Of course, since people only have one birthday each year, they would only earn extra points or extra credit that one time and not any other time.

The purpose of considering this is because it is a way to recognize and honor them. It shows the students that the teacher cares about them as individuals instead of just another class of students. This is another way to establish and to maintain mutual respect.

Also, during the first several days of school, in order to succeed in class, it is very important to show students the best ways to study the information. Of course, if the students have developed ways that work for them, so be it.

The following activity does take a little time and can be used with many subjects where there is information to be memorized. If this is a homework assignment, they can get credit for it; they can use this method of studying, and their grades can possibly improve.

For example, in foreign languages, students can take a piece of lined paper and fold it in half. They open it up so that there is a crease in the middle. They write the English words on the left side of the crease and the translation on the right side of the crease. In this way, they are actually practicing the writing of the words in English and in the foreign language, which can be much better than just reading it.

Once they have written all of the words both in English and in the foreign language, they can start memorizing the foreign language words on the right side. They can see how well they can translate those words into English, and they can check to see if they are correct.

Once they have mastered it that way, they turn to the left side of the crease where they have all of the English words. They translate the words into the foreign language and check to see if they are correct.

Using such a method is good because they can take these papers home instead of their textbook, if they only have to master the words one night or several nights. This method is far cheaper than using three by five cards and certainly less bulky to carry around.

In history classes, students can use this method for specific events with dates or specific people with duties, for example. In math classes, they can use this method for terms and specific formulas. In English classes, they can memorize their vocabulary words and literary terms with definitions.

No matter which academic class is being taught, it is always in the best interest of the high school and in the best interest of our society that students know how to spell correctly, to use appropriate grammar, and to punctuate correctly, if expressing ideas on paper is emphasized in class.

For written assignments, please consider deducting points or grades when they spell incorrectly, when they use inappropriate grammar, and when they do not punctuate well. There may be student complaints about this high expectation, but they need to be consistently doing their best in this regard in all of their classes. Eventually, they will complain less and will comply more with this request because it is really in their best interest to write well.

It would be a good idea to indicate the detention policies at the beginning of the school year, why it is given, whether it is for being tardy or for discipline problems, and how much time is determined for being tardy each time and for discipline problems. Depending upon your school's rules, it might be a good idea to allow them twenty-four hours' advanced notice about the need to serve detention so that they can adjust their schedules and so that they can notify their parents, guardians, coaches, and/or employers, if they work.

When and if there are students who have been assigned detention and they do not attend, please ask them the next school day that they attend class the reason for not showing up. If they forgot, please adhere to the school's policy in this regard. If there is not a policy in place, please consider automatically doubling their detention. If there was an emergency or if they became sick, please get a phone number of a parent or a guardian in order to verify their account for not serving detention.

No matter when it is decided to have a student serve detention, it should be at the convenience of the teacher, meaning that if he or she is only available before school, then the detention needs to be before school. If he or she is only available after school, so be it. Please remember the detention is for them and not for the teacher.

When the students do serve their detention, it is a good idea to do the following. If the detention is for being tardy, you may want to discuss how they can remedy this problem from now on, especially if it is a continuous problem.

If the detention is for being a discipline problem, discussing their reason for misbehaving and how they can remedy this problem from now on can be helpful. This discussion does not have to be lengthy, but it can be helpful for the students to understand the consequences of their actions and how to rectify the problem in the future. If they do have questions about the class, this is an ideal time. If they do not have any questions, please allow them to do their own work. Lastly, please be cognizant of how much time needs to be served, and please be punctual as to when they can leave.

In terms of dishonesty or cheating, it is interesting how our students are a reflection of our society. If people can "get away with it," it is not considered cheating, and they can rationalize these actions by saying they did not have enough time to study or the material is too difficult to learn, for example. It does not matter what reason might be given. The fact of the matter is that they are not being honest, and there are consequences for their dishonest actions.

It is vitally important to tell students from the very beginning about the need to be honest with themselves and with you. It would also be good to ask them the following: "Do you want your friends to be dishonest with you? Do you want me to give you a grade that you do not deserve? Do you want me to lower your grade because I feel like it?" After consideration of these types of questions, students will realize that cheating is inappropriate, although they truly do know.

Please mention that if they do cheat, their parents or guardians will be called. Not only are you being clear about your expectations of them, but they will understand the consequences of any possible cheating.

When and if cheating takes place, they will usually show remorse and accept their consequences. They will already know the consequences and will probably become rightfully angrier with themselves rather than with you.

Your action under these circumstances needs to be calm and firm. In this way, you are upholding certain standards of behavior. As a matter of fact, this action by them and by you can possibly lead to the real cause of their cheating so that an even better relationship and a better understanding of them can be developed, whether it is due to some personal problems they may have had or whether it be due to the fact that they may have been having difficulty with the studied material.

Please announce the following at the beginning of the school year: If something has happened outside the classroom environment that may affect their performance on quizzes and tests, please suggest to them to discuss with you privately before the graded assignment that they would like to get your permission to postpone their quizzes or tests due to a personal emergency.

This can show them that you realize that your subject is not the only thing going on in this world, that they are respected as human beings, and that they can and will be affected emotionally by circumstances that can be oftentimes beyond their control.

When and if this does occur and a postponement is granted in taking the graded assignment, please ask them when they will be prepared for it. If it is a matter of them being mildly affected physically or emotionally, it should be a matter of days. If they would have been affected a lot physically and/or emotionally, it would be a good idea to grant more time. It all depends on the circumstances.

Under these circumstances, please still emphasize to them that they still need to complete the work that the rest of the class is studying, however.

If you will allow recording in your class, announce it. If it is not allowed, please announce it.

Lastly, it is important to discuss vacations. School-designed vacations are determined to give the entire high school a much needed break for specific holidays and seasons. It is desirable for students and parents to try to organize their time to have vacations during those time slots.

If it is impossible to schedule them during these designated time slots, students need to get the assignments prior to leaving for vacation so that they can complete the work like the rest of the students. It is also the expectation that they are to complete and to turn in the work ideally prior to leaving for vacation. If not, the assignments must be turned in when they return.

Idea Number Four

An exceedingly important activity to do is to memorize at least your students' first names within the first several weeks of school, if at all possible.

Students can write their names in a seating chart, if they are in a standard classroom. If you are teaching physical education, this is more of a challenge due to having even more students than a regular academic classroom environment. They may be standing on assigned numbers inside, or they may be remaining in certain locations outside.

The importance of memorizing their first names as soon as possible at the beginning of the school year and eventually their last names is to show them that you can relate to them as individuals instead of masses of students, thus developing a better rapport with them sooner. There is then a better chance of earning their respect sooner and minimizing discipline problems sooner.

It can be an interesting and fun challenge. In a standard classroom, you could begin memorizing the students of the first row while they are working on a writing assignment. Then please memorize the second row of students' names and progress until all of the students' names in the class are memorized.

Granted, they know that it would be difficult for them to memorize one class set of names with faces, if they were in front of their own classroom. So they probably do appreciate your situation, even if they do not show it.

A side benefit of memorizing their names as soon as humanly possible is that you will learn to identify their personalities. In turn, you will lessen discipline problems from the very beginning.

There will be those students who will stand out much sooner, those being students who will test your authority and those who will do their best to convince you that they are very interested in your subject material.

It will become easier to remember all the students' names and personalities with time. It is best to be patient with yourself, but you will eventually do it.

Idea Number Five

Please consider purchasing a book of quotes on a whole range of subjects, or please do some research on the Internet for possible quotes.

On the front board of the class, please write an inspirational quote with the author's name each school day. The purpose of writing quotes on the front board can be to allow students to just read it, if they so desire, when they first arrive in the classroom. Also, they may want to apply these statements to their personal lives. By including the author's name, students may want to do some research on their own about the author, thus motivating them to read more and to be inspired even more.

If these quotes are pertinent to the subject matter, discussion of these quotes can be a part of the lesson plan. It is very well possible that some students will even look forward to coming to class in order to read the quotes.

Idea Number Six

If you are not doing so already, please consider having students organize and update a notebook regularly for the class. They can list their grades with dates on one page. They can have a section for notes with dates. They can have a section for all of their homework that is returned to them. They can have a section for their quizzes with dates. They can have a section for their tests with dates. They can also include any other pertinent sections and papers for the class. In this way, they can refer to all of the work for their class to do well in future assignments, quizzes, tests, and projects.

At the end of each grading period, it is a good idea to check their notebooks with them earning a grade or points based on what your standards are for a thorough notebook. You may want to take a part of or the entire class session while the students work on class work, study together, or do homework. Otherwise, you may want to consider taking the notebooks home to correct. The only disadvantage is that there will be many notebooks to collect and thus to evaluate at your home.

In the notebook, having a grade sheet section can be beneficial for students because they can tabulate their own grades or points, especially at the end of each grading period as you normally do. If they and you determine the same grade, they at least understand and there probably will be no hard feelings. They become responsible for their own grades, which is one of the main goals that you as their teacher want to accomplish. Grades are very important. By students having a paper with all of their grades or points, they realize how well they are doing academically.

At the time for progress reports and at the end of a grading period, please request that they determine their grades. Once they and you have determined the final grade separately, if a student determines a higher grade, it needs to be the responsibility of that individual to tactfully discuss the situation with you.

With the dated notes, if there are notes on a specific date that a student is absent, he or she can check with another student to get the notes. Also, he or she can check with you for additional information and/or clarification.

There are advantages for having separate sections for quizzes and tests. Prior to quizzes and tests, students can review those sections in order to remind themselves what they have done correctly and what they need to remember when it comes to any mistakes they may have made on these graded assignments. This can also help out prior to final exams, if your high school requires final exams.

At the start of a new grading period, please have them purge all grade sheets and homework and to retain their notes, quizzes, and tests for reference purposes in the future when they have other tests and their final exams.

Idea Number Seven

Related to homework, students need to prepare homework assignments and to study at home a lot. Some students prefer to do this by themselves. Some students prefer to work in small groups because they find working by themselves boring. They will call their study buddies. Some prefer to do a combination of both; that is, working alone and working in pairs. It would be important to mention about any peer tutoring program available at the high school. As was already mentioned, www.skype.com would be a unique way for students to connect in the virtual world of the Internet.

Many students have an interesting perspective about homework. It is only considered homework if they have to turn in written assignments. Studying to them is not considered homework, although it is something that also needs to be done for the next day's class, for the understanding of new material, for quizzes, for tests, and for projects. So the logic here is baffling, to say the least. Perhaps you can emphasize the fact that studying and written assignments are both critical homework activities, and both need to be completed for the next day's class and for successful learning.

Here are some ideas in regard to informing students about homework. First, at the beginning of class, how about having them write down their homework for the next school day instead of at the end of the class period? If not at the beginning of class, how about toward the end of class? Secondly, if your high school has a website in which teachers can post assignments, how about doing so as a reminder to students? Thirdly, another possible way to inform and/or remind them about their homework is to text or e-mail them. Whichever approach or approaches that you prefer, it is important that they know what is expected of them on a regular basis.

Many students wish to get homework "out of the way," namely by doing a hurried job at school or at home so that they have more free time for whatever is going on in their personal lives. While we all can appreciate the desire for wishing to complete homework as quickly as possible, they need to understand that doing a quick job of studying and/or completing their homework does not always equate to complete understanding in order to apply this information correctly. They need to devote quality time to do quality work, possibly resulting in a quality grade.

Even if students have difficulty with the written assignments, as long as they attempt to do them, please let them earn credit. After all, homework truly is for practice and for understanding the material to the best of their ability. If they are able to understand the work and to complete the work entirely, fine. If they are not able to understand the work but have done their best, they have tried and deserve to earn credit at least.

The following method of evaluating homework is based on how you determine their grades. If you assign points, fine. If you assign grades, fine. For the following explanation, there will be a reference to grades, but please consider either full points, no points, or half points, if you assign points.

Please consider the following in terms of evaluating their written assignments. Every time the students complete a written homework assignment, it is either an A or a red F. An A is for a written homework assignment in which they do the best they can.

If it is not done at all, you can ask them if there is any particular reason why it was not completed. If they were simply lazy or forgot to complete their written homework, they automatically earn a red F, which is an easily identifiable way to determine what assignments are missing due to their irresponsibility. They will usually be very honest about this. If they continuously make up excuses for not completing their homework, it is best to inform them that you will call their parents. If there are unique circumstances, please be flexible with them, but they still need to complete their graded work just like everybody else.

If the student has been sick or if there has been an emergency of some sort, please excuse them from doing the assignment with the expectation that they are to complete that particular assignment and also the assignment that might be given that day for the next school day.

During the time students study a particular unit, if there are any red Fs, they can make up the work and earn half credit, resulting in a C, because a red F and an A will be a C. It is best to inform them if they have any red Fs prior to the end of a particular unit. In this way, if they do, they have the responsibility to make up the missing work; however, they cannot make up the red Fs after the major unit test.

The homework for a particular chapter is so that they can practice using the information of that chapter in order to be more successful for quizzes and the test of that chapter. It is a waste of time and effort to complete any red Fs after the unit is completed, and the class has moved on to the next chapter.

When the students have completed all of their assignments, either on time ideally or made up for a C prior to a major test, their overall grade at the end of the grading period is increased: for example, C to C+ or B+ to an A−.

If they would have even one or two missing assignments at the end of a grading period, their grade would not increase. For every two red Fs after the first two red Fs at the end of the grading period, their grade would decrease: for example, C+ to C or A− to B+.

Thus, they would understand the importance of completing their homework in a timely manner. It also shows that they can be respected as human beings having forgetful and/or lazy moments and to be allowed time to make up the work prior to the major chapter test, but only for half credit.

There is another way to look at homework. Let's say that you had been sick the previous school night, or there might have been an emergency so that you could not complete the correcting of work that was promised to the students to have been completed by the next day. We are all human, and things happen. The flexibility that students have for us when we cannot fulfill our obligation needs to be considered for them.

While homework is a necessary ingredient of student learning, it can be very helpful to not assign homework once in a while. Let's say they have had a major test on a Tuesday. Please consider not assigning homework that night in order to give them an opportunity to relax in regard to your class. The reason is that they may have felt a lot of stress already resulting from taking a major test, and this is a well-deserved gift to them. A side benefit of doing this can be that they will be more receptive to learning new information the next school day.

If they have been so overwhelmed with homework in the class during the week and if more work is assigned on a Friday for the following school day, that can result in students not learning very well and/or having a bad attitude about you and the subject. If they are given no homework on a Friday, they will be relieved, and they may become that much more effective and refreshed the following school day.

If it is unavoidable that you need to state on Friday in class that the students are going to have an essay, a quiz, a test, or a project the following week, please consider having it due not the next school day, but due on the second day of school the following week. Of course, if this is not possible due to time constraints of one form or another, then this is not a possibility.

There is another viewpoint about homework that needs to be addressed. There are debates as to whether homework should be assigned. After all, students learn a lot of information and oftentimes apply that information quite well in class already. Thus, there are teachers who simply prefer not requiring homework and thus letting students bear the responsibility to study on their own. A nice residual effect would be that teachers do not have to assign homework, nor do they have to correct homework. Of course, these teachers still have quizzes and tests.

So whatever your viewpoint may be about homework, whether you assign no homework, some homework, or a lot of homework, the goal of all teachers is to have their students learn the information to the best of their ability. Nevertheless, students do need some regular practice with the information.

Idea Number Eight

Homework requests may be available at your school and are for students not attending school for a short or an extended period of time due to illness, for example. After filling out and turning in the appropriate form, students can complete these assignments at home.

If such homework requests would not be available at your school, please consider calling, e-mailing, or texting these absent students with the details of their missed assignments.

Please also consider calling them to see how they are feeling, to see if they are making any progress on the homework, and to deal with any of their questions. Also, when talking with them, please mention to them to turn in any assignments that are requested on the day they return so that they can catch up with the rest of the class. Of course, this would be dependent upon the reason for their absence. If they have had an accident that requires much physical attention and less time can be devoted to homework, it is desirable to be more flexible as to when they are able to concentrate well enough in order to turn in their assignments.

As for taking any quizzes and/or tests under these circumstances, you need to work with these particular students in order to find out when they can take them when they return to class. Seeing that they will have other classes with possible quizzes and/or tests to complete, it may take some time. Nevertheless, you and they need to determine specific dates and times when these graded assignments can be completed.

Idea Number Nine

Teachers typically phone the students' parents or guardians at home when there are academic and/or discipline problems of the students in the classroom. This is extremely important in order to maintain open communication between parents or guardians, students, and teachers and to possibly help to alleviate these types of problems.

Please mention to the students in class that positive phone calls will be made to their parents or guardians at home during the first several months of the new school year. Please choose one student in each of your classes each school night, which is typically Sunday through Thursday nights. Also, phone calls should take place only when a homework assignment is given since part of the purpose for making these types of phone calls is to make sure that the homework assignments are being brought home and are being completed.

An average teacher has five to six classes a day, unless it is the block schedule where there are typically four classes. So five or six phone calls could be made each school night. The rationale behind this is to not over-burden yourself with many phone calls each school night. In turn, it will be easier to handle in this way instead of making a dozen or more phone calls each school night because you have personal and professional obligations to fulfill, let alone the need to take it easy!

When talking with the parents or guardians, please introduce yourself, the importance of the class, and the expectations of the class and see whether or not they have any questions. Then please ask if their young adults have their study materials for your class (textbook, notebook, and/or homework) at home. In that eventuality, they earn extra points or an extra A. If their young adult is there, he or she can show the parents or guardians the study materials.

If the young adult is not present, please ask the parents or guardians to find out if the study materials are there upon his or her return home. In turn, they can write a note and have their young adult bring it to school so that you can mark the points or extra A. The parents or guardians would thus confirm or deny that their young adult had the appropriate study materials.

If their young adult does not have the study materials at home when he or she is there or when he or she returns, it is a wake-up call for the student to bring the study materials home in order to prepare for the next school day on a regular basis, and it is a wake-up call to the parents or guardians that their young adult needs to be more conscientious about bringing study materials home on a regular basis. Under those circumstances, no extra points or grade would be given.

If you get an answering machine, please call back some other time so that you can actually talk to one of the parents or guardians.

If for any reason these phone calls cannot be made consistently due to your obligations, there is no urgency to accomplish all of the phone calling within a given time period. If it takes a longer time than thought, fine. The idea is that the lines of communication with the parents or guardians are open for the benefit of their young adults and the parents or guardians.

It will be apparent after a while that the students will actually ask when you will be calling their homes, which is a rarity!

Please also call the students' homes sometime during the school year if there is a major improvement by them on a quiz, a test, a project, in their behavior, and/or in their attitude.

There is a major domino effect that can take place due to making these positive phone calls. The parents or guardians can become startled that a school official calls to give a personal message that is positive because they may be so accustomed to negative phone calls from the school. They will realize that you care about their young adults and that you are proud of their accomplishments.

This can result in a better relationship between parents or guardians and you. This can result in a better relationship within the family structure. This can result in a better relationship between your students and you. This ultimately can possibly result in better behaved classes and improvement in their grades. The positive ramifications for everyone are endless and indeed can be very inspiring.

Idea Number Ten

There will always be times, for instance on a Friday, when even the best of classes can become rowdy, and the noise level will become intolerable. You can speak loudly, and even that sometimes will not get their attention.

While most students most of the time will respond to your request to calm down and to be cooperative, what can be done when they disregard your request to be quiet and to be cooperative?

Please consider using the soft speaking technique with a rowdy class. Please talk in a much lower voice than usual in front of the class. The students will realize that if they are to continue talking, they will miss out on some important information. They probably will stop in order to listen. They will understand quite well that they are talking out of turn. Then the lesson plan can be resumed.

Idea Number Eleven

If the soft speaking technique seems to be unsuccessful, please still refuse to shout to get their attention. Instead, please stand in front of the class being totally silent, and please pretend to be writing something on a piece of paper while looking at them. Eventually, students will realize that you are being silent for a reason. They will not know what to expect, if their citizenship grades are being lowered (if citizenship grades are given) or if their names are being written down for detention and/or student referrals. They will probably become silent, thus allowing you to continue with your lesson plan. You don't have to comment about what is being written, even if they ask.

Idea Number Twelve

If a class misbehaves a lot so that regular instruction is secondary, the chair idea can certainly draw a lot of attention. An empty chair is placed in front of the class facing the students. The comment can be made that since there are certain individuals who wish to have all of the attention, thus distracting the purpose of the class, they have a choice. One misbehaving student will be invited to sit in the chair, and he or she can remain seated there for twenty minutes. He or she obviously wants all of the attention, and this is the best way to handle this need. Then the next misbehaving student can take his or her place after twenty minutes for another twenty minutes. While seated facing the class, they need to focus their attention on the lesson plan, and they need to remain quiet.

The other option for these individual students is to sit with the other students and to cooperate in the best possible way so that the normal work of the class can be accomplished so that they may be better informed.

More than likely, students will choose to remain in their own seats and to cooperate better.

The students will realize very well that you mean business, and you do not have to raise your voice. It is important to be firm, but especially calm.

If this approach is used, if it is effective, and if they begin to be uncooperative again, by simply placing the chair in front of the class or leaving it there with you pointing to the chair can be quite sufficient to calm the class down very nicely and very quickly.

Idea Number Thirteen

A-B activities can apply to any class in which the students can formulate questions that have one specific answer for each question.

Let's take a Spanish class, for example. They have studied a list of words already. For homework, they write down three words in English with the appropriate translations. After checking it off that they have completed this the next day, the students line up in two lines facing one another.

There is the A line of students, and there is the B line of students. The A students ask their three words in English to be translated by the B line of students. Then the B line asks their questions of the A line. Afterward, the A line of students moves to the next person, and they continue. The student at the end of the A line then comes to the beginning of the line. This activity continues in this same fashion until they have been questioned by the entire line.

Meantime, you can circulate among the students to have them remain on task and to answer any questions they may have.

You and the students will find this exercise to be an effective tool for learning. They can feel that they are experts of the words that they present, and they become that much more aware of other words that are presented to them by the other students with the ultimate goal of everyone being able to improve in future homework assignments, quizzes, and tests.

Idea Number Fourteen

The slate game is a great way to actively involve students with the studied material.

Slate boards should be large enough so that students can write their answers on it because if there are students in the back of your classroom, it is important that their writing is large enough so that the slates can be read.

While chalk can be used with slate boards, they do create a lot of dust on the desks and on the students' clothing, and there may be people who are allergic to chalk as well. Thus, it would be a good idea to have slate boards with current marker boards that can be found in today's typical classroom. Marker pens of different colors can be purchased along with cut-up different pieces of cloth so that students are able to erase their slate boards.

If purchasing slate boards, markers, and cloths is out of the question due to budgetary constraints, please have the students use their standard writing paper in which they can write their answers in big letters. They should use dark pens or pencils that can be read very easily.

For the rest of the explanation of this activity, let's use the term "slate game," but if you need to use paper instead with your students, please substitute the word "paper(s)" for "slate(s)." Also, if paper is utilized, please ask your students to write answers on both sides of each paper in order to save paper and to save the environment.

For the slate game activity half of the time please allow the students to select their own groups of students whom they want in their rows of typically five or six students per row, if you have large classes. Please make sure that the students have balanced rows so that there are not six in one row and four in another row. Under these circumstances, one student from the row of six students would be requested to move to the row where there are four students. Basically, they know who the better students are.

The other half of the time for the slate game, you can select the students for the competition rows. It is then best to try to put a cross section of students in each row, meaning placing students that usually excel with students who have difficulties understanding the information. Again, the rows should be equal amounts of students.

Prior to the slate game activity please allow them time to review the material for five minutes in their rows either individually and/or in pairs. Then they can ask any questions. Once you've answered their last-minute questions, the slate game can begin.

Please have them distribute the slate boards, the markers, and the cloths to each other. If you are asking them to use their own paper and pen or pencil, please ask them to take out those materials.

You should announce the following to the students. One condition for the slate game activity is that they are to do their own work. If any student chooses to cheat by looking at someone else's slate board for the answer or asking another student for the answer, that student's row is disqualified for that possible point. Also, if your school gives citizenship grades like excellent, satisfactory, or unsatisfactory, please consider giving that student an unsatisfactory grade for the entire grading period. Honesty is the best policy!

The entire class can be asked how to say a vocabulary word, a grammar word, a sentence in the foreign language studied in this class, or about any concept that they are studying in the class. If it is a vocabulary word, it is suggested to value it as one point. If it is a grammar word, it is suggested to value it as two points. If it is a sentence, it is suggested to value it as three points.

Once all the students have written their response and have placed the slates face down, you begin with the first row to find out their response for the first question. If they do have the correct answer, they earn the value of the question (vocabulary word, grammar word, or sentence), which is marked on the front board under row one. If one or more students in one row has an incorrect answer, the row does not earn the point or points.

Let's say if the first row does not get the point or points due to one or more incorrect answers, the teacher proceeds to the second row. If their row is completely correct, they get the point or points.

The second row gets the second question. The third row gets the third question. Thus, each row has an equal opportunity to answer with their response.

Once the teacher asks questions of all the rows, the slate game continues with the first row, and it continues playing in this fashion for the majority of the class period.

In the eventuality that none of the rows gets the correct answer due to the fact that one or more students had an incorrect answer in each row, it is a good idea to ask the entire class what the answer is. Surely, there will be at least one or more students who will have the correct answer.

You might consider giving students some goofy clues. This would help them remember words better when it comes time for their quizzes and tests. So any way that the slate game can be livened up, the material will actually be engrained that much more so, with hopefully that much better results in their graded work.

It is a good idea to judge how much time is remaining in the class so that questions can be asked of all the rows prior to the end of the class. In other words, for example, it is important not to end a slate game activity with row number three when there are six rows because everyone should have an equal opportunity of answering.

At the end of the class period, please allow enough time for the students to return the slate game items to the areas where they are normally stored. If they have been using paper, please have a recycling box for them.

Prior to excusing them to leave class, please excuse them by rows in order to make sure that each row is clean for the next class.

If a slate game is scheduled for more than one day or if it is noticed that a majority of the students still need more time for slate game activities to feel more comfortable with the information, please try to include an additional day. The idea is that they learn and practice the information.

Please consider giving extra credit or extra points for the upcoming quiz or test to the two top rows. If there would be a tie for first place, then there could conceivably be three rows earning extra credit for that quiz or test.

Idea Number Fifteen

Many teachers allow students to give presentations to the rest of the class. It can be a valuable tool.

Please let them earn the maximum amount of points or an A on this project for several reasons. First of all, while some students may feel comfortable presenting information in front of their peers, some may not, and they actually may make mistakes, no matter how well prepared they are. Secondly, even if students feel confident and at ease in front of the class, evaluating their presentations can be rather subjective and open for debate, unless a very well-defined method of assessing each component of their work is determined.

If one or several of the students would be absent the day of their presentations, the next time that there are presentations, their grade for that presentation could be doubled.

A lot of teachers have their students form their own groups in class. The teachers assign specific aspects of a unit. After working together for a class period or two maximum, they present a lesson to the class for a specific amount of minutes. They can use any technique they wish so long as it is presented with good taste. They can use the teacher's board, if they so desire. It is important for them to present their ideas in a visual way (poster boards, on the board, and PowerPoint, for example), which will keep the attention of the rest of the class help in learning and retaining the information.

During and after the presentation, the rest of the class can ask pertinent questions so that they can understand the information more clearly. Lastly, it is suggested that the presenters give a practice quiz that does not count for a grade or for points to the rest of the students based on the supplied information and discuss the answers afterward.

This is a great technique so that students can learn from one another. They can become the authorities, which can result in more learning, and there can be an additional benefit of better self-esteem. If they do not understand a particular concept very well, please clarify for all concerned.

Idea Number Sixteen

Every semester as time permits, please allow students to make up their own groups and to work on a theme based on the general aspects of your subject for a video project that can be produced by them. The ideal is to have the video presented on a television monitor, if they have a video camera. If they do not have access to a video camera, they need to present their play in front of the class.

Once the groups have determined what they want to do after usually one or two class periods and once they get your permission to present that particular theme, they need to be allotted approximately a month to complete a video or a skit in front of the class in which they completely make up their own dialogues. Everyone needs to participate equally. The video project or the class skit should last seven to ten minutes and could be evaluated on the length, the creativity, and anything else that you believe is pertinent to the class and to their presented themes.

There should be some qualifications for the video and for the presentation. First, whatever topic they choose cannot be offensive to anyone in the class. After all, you do not want to have any complaints brought to the administration by parents, guardians, or students. Secondly, each group needs to give you their videos or the written dialogues for the presentation so that they can be reviewed by you prior to the presentation in class. The reason for this is because the dialogue and the action still need to be assessed to be sure that there is nothing offensive to anyone at all.

In the event there are any videos and plays that may be objectionable or offensive, you can simply indicate your decision not to have that particular video presented or play acted in class, and if they wish to present these objectionable videos and/or skits to students of the class, they need to make arrangements with anyone who wishes to view them before or after school, but not during class time and not in your class. They still earn their grade or their points, however. You can explain to those particular students what your decision is and your explanation, if you so desire.

This is a great tool for students to use their own creativity in fun ways in order to work with the information that they have been learning in the classroom, as well as to have it count as a major grade or to earn points for them.

Of course, there can be conflicts in schedules for various reasons among the students for making progress on such a project; however, all of the students can be successful in completing it, even for the students who normally do not do well in class. It can actually increase the chances of inspiring underachieving students to want to learn. They will learn how to become more self-reliant and more dependent upon others, when appropriate, so that they can work as a team. So it can be a very positive experience, and they can have a great time sharing the videos or seeing the plays in the front of the class when they are due.

This video project idea would be ideal for many classes. A natural for this type of activity is for drama classes that can write and produce these presentations. Many English classes dealing with literature can certainly liven up their readings by acting the parts of different characters in books and adding their creative twists in the process.

Business teachers might want to utilize this method so that the students can act like billionaires in the business world and also pretend to make profitable investments.

Science teachers might want to utilize the video project idea so that the students can re-create experiments done by scientists or act like famous scientists throughout the ages.

History teachers certainly can use this approach depicting scenes of history and depicting many historical figures.

ROTC classes can pretend to be their teachers, focusing on how to clean a rifle or going on a field trip, for example.

The agriculture classes can demonstrate how to take care of their crops and/or their animals. Maybe, to add a little humor, they can add dialogues that these animals would share among themselves and with humans.

The home economic classes can demonstrate how to cook. This project might be a little costly since they probably would need food, which they would have to buy.

The special education students can also have a lot of fun and learn about one of their many subjects. They could act like their teachers or pretend to be billionaires, for example.

If the students feel very proud of their work, they may even wish to present it on www.youtube.com, if they so desire.

Who knows? There might even be some future writers, producers, directors, actors, actresses, makeup artists, and set designers that might become inspired to enter the film or play industry, just because the video project or class skit is required of them . . .

Idea Number Seventeen

Since the youth of today are so familiar with television programs and DVDs, it can be an advantage with some qualifications. Once you have previewed the television programs and DVDs that are relevant to the subject matter in order to make sure that they do not contain anything that can be considered inappropriate, please ask the department chair and the administration if they will approve of you showing any of these to the class. If so, they could be presented, and their importance could be discussed as a class or as an analysis by each student as to their judgment of the work and if there were any special themes presented.

If having a field trip to a local movie theater is possible, this is the ideal; if this is an impossibility, perhaps a movie at the theaters can be assigned as an extra credit activity. Again, it would be best that they write an analysis.

It is very well possible that students can learn that much more about the subject matter from television programs, DVDs, and movies along with book learning and exercises that are assigned to them.

Idea Number Eighteen

Since we always want our students to improve, please consider the C+ or higher enticement. If the entire class earns a C+ or higher on a quiz or a test, they have no homework one night.

If the entire class earns a B– or higher on a quiz or a test, they have no homework for one week.

If the entire class earns an A– or higher on a quiz or a test, they have no homework for two weeks.

Even if one student would earn a grade a little bit lower than what is expected for no homework for a particular time period, the class would not have the reward being offered. If that would occur, it could be mentioned that they were very close, and they could be encouraged to try that much harder by studying a little bit more so that they could possibly earn the appropriate reward the next time.

If there would be any students who are absent the day of the quiz or the test and if the rest of the class has earned one of the enticements to improve, the rest of the class needs to wait for these individual students to take the quiz or the test.

Should you have two or more classes of the same preparation, all of these classes would have to attain that expectation in order to earn the appropriate reward. The reason for having this expectation is that it would be difficult to have separate preparations with one class having reached that goal and the other class not.

Ultimately, it is positive peer pressure to help all the students prepare for their graded work and improve, which is what all teachers hope for. It shows students that you as their teacher have confidence in them having the capability to improve, which can result in better learning, better grades, and fewer discipline problems.

Generally speaking, there will be more times in which a class will earn the C+ or higher enticement, and there may be times that a class may earn the B– or A– or higher enticement, based on the caliber and the motivation of the students involved.

Idea Number Nineteen

There are four types of quizzes that you might or might not be using in the classroom already and that are very effective.

Students like to have some sort of control even during a classroom setting. For homework, please have them make up a quiz for one another with the same amount of questions that are normally posted on the quizzes. The next day, the quiz is checked off as a homework assignment.

After five minutes of studying, the students exchange quizzes and take each other's quizzes. Afterward, they return and correct the quizzes by having a separate sheet of paper including the answers.

This is a very useful tool to help them remember the information and avoid more mistakes, if at all possible, on future graded work. This type of quiz is just for practice and is not like a graded quiz.

Here is a second type of quiz to be considered. On the day of the quiz, please allow them to study five minutes in class. Then, two practice quizzes are given and consist of a certain amount of words or ideas in each quiz out of which some words or ideas will actually be on the quiz that the students will be taking.

The purpose of giving these practice quizzes is to have them feel more comfortable with the material on the day of the graded quiz. They then study for another five minutes, and they need to get rid of these practice quizzes before taking the actual quiz.

Instead of you writing down the correct answers for each quiz, please circle each of the incorrect answers. In this way, when they get their quizzes back, they will need to pay attention as to what all of the correct answers are for the next homework assignment. If they have made no mistakes whatsoever, they do not have to do this assignment. They automatically earn an A for this assignment.

For students who have one or more incorrect answers, for homework, please have them write down the word or question once and the correct answer five times. For those students who made mistakes, they would be evaluated on this homework assignment in the following manner:

0 errors = A
1 error = A–
2 errors = B+
3 errors = B
4 errors = B–
5 errors = C+
6 errors = C
7 errors = C–
8 errors = D+
9 errors = D
10 errors = D–
11 errors or more = F

The purpose of this activity is to make sure that they understand all of the words or ideas very well so that the missed words or ideas would be understood by them for future graded work. This counts as a graded homework assignment and not a quiz assignment.

The last type of quiz to consider is a voluntary graded assignment initiated by the students. As long as they are studying a particular unit, please allow them to take an extra quiz on any concept, vocabulary, or grammar words.

If they wish to do this, there are some things for them to be aware of. First of all, this is a voluntary graded quiz, and they need to study well. Secondly, they need to ask when you are available on a specific day outside classroom time since class time is devoted to all of the students' education. Thirdly, after taking the quiz, they must turn it in. When they take the quiz, it counts as a grade. In other words, should they not feel good about the quiz after taking the quiz, they could not say that they prefer not to have the quiz count.

They can only take one extra quiz a day because it can be tremendously difficult to correct a multitude of extra quizzes from one student, let alone from many students each day. Under these circumstances, you would truly not be able to keep up with the regular work.

In this way, students are able to have more control of their own grade. More than likely, they will tend to take these extra quizzes prior to the end of a grading period in order to improve their overall grade, if necessary. It usually would be a good idea to offer this possibility up until three days prior to the end of the grading period because the normal assignments and grades are coming in and their total grades need to be determined. After all, you do not want to be inundated with any more work than you have to at the end of the grading period.

Idea Number Twenty

Please consider notifying your students via phone, via texting, and/or via e-mailing of their grades on quizzes, tests, projects, and quarter and final grades at the end of the grading period. Ask them to write down their phone number or e-mail address on top of the quiz or test or on a sheet of paper that would be distributed to them. Then, after determining the grade, they can be notified. It can take just a minute or two of your time, but it can brighten their day, if they have done well. If they have not done so well, it is important to accentuate the fact that they can learn from their mistakes in order to improve their understanding and ultimately their grades.

You probably will find that about one-third of your students will take advantage of this offer. Otherwise, most students will choose to wait for their grades until the next school day because they basically know what kind of grade they are earning or they just simply can wait until the next class session.

Whether they wish to be notified or not, they will realize that you care about them as individuals.

Idea Number Twenty-One

There are many teachers who believe that when students have earned high grades, this is the reward within itself; it is intrinsic in nature. They believe that giving certificates and/or extra privileges at the high school level is too much of an elementary school level technique. Indeed, this may be the case; however, we are dealing with young adults who need extrinsic rewards. They personally need to be awarded for their accomplishments.

If you agree that there is no need to give certificates, your opinion is to be respected. If you agree that there is a need to give certificates, the rest of this idea is for your consideration.

Let's face it. In the "real world," adults are oftentimes recognized for their achievements with salary increases and in ceremonies.

After major tests, please hand out certificates consisting of different colors so that they stand out. The first, second, and third place certificate winners can typically be the same students; however, there can be some notable exceptions at times because the students who are on the verge of earning these certificates want to be recognized as well. These certificates can be motivating factors for those students who also want to be recognized. Thus, many will attempt and possibly even succeed. Ultimately, no matter how much improvement they may make, they will be more receptive to learning, one of the goals for teachers.

Please also distribute certificates of improvement to students who have improved since their previous test. For example, even if they improved slightly from an F to a D–, from a C to C+, or dramatically from a C to an A, they could earn certificates of improvement with their names on it. Again, motivation to want to improve their knowledge of your subject can become a great reward for them by their actual improvement.

These certificates of improvement would be valuable to them because if they were to earn two certificates of improvement during a given grading period, their overall grade at the end of the grading period would increase a notch; for example, from a B to a B+ or a B+ to an A–.

Idea Number Twenty-Two

On the other hand, for those students who earn grades ranging from a D+ to an F on a major test, please develop a form letter including some suggestions as to how to study better and how to get extra help from you and perhaps from the peer tutoring program at your school. Please encourage your students to read this letter. Also, please encourage them to give this letter to their parents or guardians.

If the students would return the letter signed by one of the parents or guardians within two school days, then the students could earn an extra A as a quiz grade with their other grades or extra points to be added to their overall points.

This test letter idea can help, based on the desire to improve of the students themselves and based on the support and the desire of the parents and/or guardians.

When students continuously fail to complete their assignments and when they continuously fail their quizzes and major tests, please call them at their homes since they will not have to confront you, and this activity may appear less threatening for them. Also, without anyone present, they can reflect on what they are doing more.

Idea Number Twenty-Three

After reaching them by phone, please ask them to repeat after you: "I," and they say "I." Then you say "want," and they say "want." Then you say "to," and they say "to." Then, you ask them to say "fail." While they might say "I want to," they normally will not say the word "fail." In fact, they generally will say "I don't want to fail." Then they can be asked why they are failing, and they may begin to reveal what is bothering them.

Sometimes this activity will work, and sometimes it will not work. It is totally an individual matter.

Idea Number Twenty-Four

Many teachers are so inundated with their regular responsibilities that they have no time for extra credit work by students. If that is the case, you are totally in your right not to include additional work. Also, many teachers believe that if students were to do their regular work, they would not have to complete extra credit assignments in order to possibly boost their grades. Again, this is very logical to believe and to be respected.

Indeed, extra credit does require extra work, if and when the students attempt these assignments. Nevertheless, if some students just simply cannot understand the basic information and if they are allowed a means to think differently while still being involved in the subject matter, it can be a way to inspire students to not only complete extra credit work, but perhaps also to improve their understanding of the subject and possibly their grades.

If extra credit assignments are available for your students, it is a good idea to give them an extra credit sheet at the beginning of the school year that contains somewhat easy to very challenging assignments. Please consider mentioning to them that if they choose to do any of these extra credit assignments, it does not necessarily mean that they automatically earn extra credit, and they are responsible to do their own work without your assistance. It has to be great quality extra credit to earn credit for their work. In terms of the actual value of these extra credit assignments, this needs to be based on your judgment.

Since each subject and each teacher will be different, if you are so inclined to offer extra credit, please let your mind ponder the possibilities of extra credit ideas.

As for foreign language classes, here are some possibilities to consider:

1. Prepare a meal based on the country of your foreign language for the entire class.
2. With another student, prepare and present a five-minute skit by memory in your foreign language in front of the class.
3. Call the embassy of the country of your foreign language so that a representative can come to the class to present different aspects of this studied culture. Then write an analysis as to what you have learned. If you are in level one or two, it may be in English. If you are in level three or higher, it must be in the foreign language being studied.

In regard to Back-To-School Night functions, please announce to your students that if their parents, guardians, or any other immediate adult family member can attend to find out about their young adults' progress in your class, their young adults can earn extra credit for the next major test.

Generally speaking, the Back-To-School functions can result in that many more family members attending, a better understanding of what is going on in your class, and even better student cooperation. Even if you choose to make the positive phone calls at the beginning of the school year, these parents can actually see what is being done in the class and see you.

Idea Number Twenty-Five

The camp idea at a mountain retreat related to school can be a great way to involve students and teachers outside the school environment. It could last a weekend depending upon how much is desired to be accomplished and based on the following factors.

If interested, approval from the administration on the school site level as well as from the district administration needs to be granted. The costs for each student based on a specific number of students needs to be determined. Will the school and/or the district support the costs, or will the students' parents or guardians need to pay partially or totally? If the students need to pay, what kinds of fund-raising events can be organized? Bus transportation or parents transporting students to the campsite and return needs to be arranged. Maybe food preparation classes could be invited to cook meals. The appropriate insurance forms and parent permission forms need to be distributed and filled out completely, in the event of any accidents.

Support from teachers from your school site's department is important, and please include other high schools in your school district and outside your school district, if a minimum amount of students will be needed and cannot be acquired at your high school. Chaperones and security will be needed as well.

The teachers involved in this project need to discuss how many credits can be earned and how the students' grades will be determined with your administration. Perhaps the actual amount of hours in instructional activities can be important to determine the quantity of credits. As for their grades, it is a good idea to divide up the amount of students based on how many teachers are involved and based on how much interaction each teacher will have with those particular students. No matter which group of students the teachers have, the teachers need to assess their students in the same fashion, and this needs to be expressed to the students themselves at a meeting with them prior to the camp in the form of a contract regarding grades and their behavior.

As for dividing up the groups of students, it is best to consider their ability or their knowledge of this subject matter. In other words, it would be beneficial to have students with no knowledge of this subject matter in one group but not with an advanced group of students.

If and when you consider the camp idea, students who are mature enough for this type of experience are more than likely better behaved compared to those students who like to create problems in the classroom. Normally, students who behave inappropriately will not wish to consider the camp idea anyway.

There is a lot to be done for this type of activity; however, the benefits for all of your students far outweigh any work that needs to be done. Maybe a lot of the students wishing to attend can help in some way. The more teachers that are involved in this camp idea, the less that any one particular teacher has to do as a result.

The camp idea is applicable to many subjects.

If you are a foreign language teacher, the importance of being able to communicate and to understand more about the culture involved always need to be emphasized. Groups can be divided according to their levels of proficiency. Perhaps students who have never studied the target language can be welcomed. There can be arts and crafts activities. There can be sports of the studied language and culture. Students can learn dances of the studied language and culture, if there are teachers who know how to folk dance. Walking and identifying parts of nature in the target language can be considered. There can be meals consisting of that language's culture.

The basic requirement and expectation for all students and all teachers is that everyone speaks in the target language. Of course, in the event of an illness or an emergency, those students and you most definitely need to speak in English.

The camp idea is an appropriate activity for geology classes so that students may study land formations along with maps of the area where the camp class takes place. Perhaps geologists could possibly attend to give that much more insight into the area.

For English classes, students could possibly read novels and/or plays prior to camp to discuss their viewpoints in groups at the camp. Then they may want to play the parts of the different characters involved. Perhaps local and/or nationally recognized actors and actresses could be invited to attend to present monologues, to present plays, and/or to answer questions from students.

The Academic Decathlon requires a lot of studying throughout the calendar year, and incorporating the camp idea with students over a weekend, several weekends, or even during a week of vacation can be very helpful for these students. Perhaps guest speakers knowledgeable in the studies of the Academic Decathlon can be invited to speak and to answer questions from students.

Physical education classes may want to utilize the camp idea by requiring students to hike, to swim, and to run.

Perhaps home economic classes could attend the above camps in order to learn about cooking from local chefs. Also, it could be considered to have these students cook for other students.

Idea Number Twenty-Six

First and foremost, time needs to be devoted to administering an organized program of study in which students are able to learn the information in class. While you need to do this with a majority of your students, there may be students who are far advanced in their ability to grasp ideas and are able to excel. In fact, they may be bored because the class seems to be going so slowly from their perspective. Of course, if you have enough to do to manage your class's education and do not wish to bother with independent study, that is totally understandable.

If your school administration allows individual students to advance at their own rate, this is a fabulous way for them and for teachers to work together and also both to become that much more inspired.

In order to begin the process of independent study, there needs to be the teacher's willingness to permit students to pursue this type of study. Secondly, there needs to be the willingness of the students themselves who are self-motivators, are very intelligent, do not need much direction all the time, are mature, and do not create discipline problems. There probably is some sort of contract that needs to be filled out in detail with the appropriate signatures and that probably can be acquired from the administration. There also needs to be specific expectations about how frequently the two of you will meet and by when all the work will need to be completed.

It is exceptionally important to indicate that they are responsible to follow the contract as close as possible, or the contract will be invalid.

Upon completion of the independent study work, please be sure to determine the grade earned so that the contract can be turned in to the administration and to the students involved prior to the end of the semester.

There may be students on independent study who may complete all of the assigned work, quizzes, tests, and projects well in advance of the determined deadline. They may actually be able to earn a year's worth of credits in a semester. It all depends on the students involved.

Please involve yourself with independent study only sparingly because it does require special attention and more time on your part.

You may have independent study students who can work on their own in your classroom, and if so, they need to work by themselves without being a distraction to the rest of the students. Usually, this will be the case.

If these independent study students want to take your class but cannot fit your class into their schedule, they will need to work with their counselor so that they can take this subject while you are teaching another class. For your own sake, please do not have these students during your preparation period because time needs to be devoted to catching up on your work, reproducing papers, and making phone calls, for example. Also, it is important for you to have your time to be away from students just for a while.

During the class period that you have these independent study students, please make it a point to ask them each day whether they have any questions. They are expected to turn in homework on a regular basis so that you may correct it to give them feedback. If they intend to take a quiz or a test the next day, they need to inform you so that you can have the graded assignment available by the next day.

Idea Number Twenty-Seven

Let's say there is a test on a Thursday, and the test takes a long time to correct. Indeed, it will take even more time on Friday and perhaps during the weekend. Under these circumstances, please consider mentioning to the students that Friday's class will be light in general.

That can mean any of the following possibilities. First, on Friday, students can be asked how they felt about the test and to ask questions. By asking an open-ended question like this, you are allowing that much more communication with them, and you are showing that much more respect for them.

Secondly, if you would want to, some general concepts of the next chapter could be introduced but without them taking any notes. It would be just to relate to them what they will be studying.

Thirdly, you could say on Thursday that they can bring any homework for any other classes to class so that they can complete their work in order to make your class period a study hall for them. They could work individually or in pairs, but they would be expected to be working. Should they not have any homework or any studying to do for any of their classes, they would be required to read something of their own choosing.

Should the majority of the class take advantage of your kind offer by becoming a discipline problem, then you would begin a new lesson based on the new chapter, and there would be homework assigned due for Monday. Thus, you are placing the responsibility onto the students to be mature and to use the time wisely and well. More than likely, students are wise enough to want to use the time well so that they can focus on their homework either individually and/or in pairs so that they have little or no homework for themselves during the weekend.

While they would be working individually and/or in pairs, you could devote time to your own work so that you could hopefully have less school responsibilities during the weekend, which is always a good thing. So it can be a win-win situation for the students as well as for yourself.

If you would be working on the tests of the students in the class, perhaps they could find out their grades as their tests are completely evaluated. You may even want to call individual students to come to your desk so that you could correct it and answer any questions they may have.

Another activity to consider that would be good for English and foreign language classes is the circle paragraph idea on a Friday. English students would do this exercise in English, while the students studying a foreign language would do this exercise in that foreign language.

The students are asked to rearrange the chairs so that they are seated in a circle. They take out a piece of paper, and they write their name on it on the upper right side. On the first line, they write down the following: "Once upon a time" either in English or in the foreign language. Then they fill in the rest of that first sentence only. Afterward, they pass their paper to the right, and that student reads the first sentence and writes a second sentence. They continue doing this until they eventually get their own paper back. At that point in time, the students read the stories that have been based on the perspectives of the entire class. This is a fun activity that can last all or part of the class period based on the size of the class. You could determine different topic sentences that would generate their creativity.

Idea Number Twenty-Eight

Many high schools require final exams at the end of each semester so that teachers can determine how much information their students truly do understand and so that those students who attend a higher institution of learning will be able to feel more comfortable with comprehensive semester final exams. Indeed, this idea has a lot of merit, although it can create a lot of stress for all concerned due to the fact that these final exams can weigh heavily on the overall grade in the class based on department and school standards for percentages for semester final exams.

Since final exams are a reflection of what has been learned during a semester, there are some high schools that allow students who already have an A or A– going into the final exam the option of not taking the final exam. If your high school has that option available for your students, please take advantage of it for several reasons. First of all, this will create less stress for those particular students who have excelled already, thus allowing them the opportunity to study for their other final exams. Of course, they may not have to take any of their final exams, if they have excelled in all of their classes. In that eventuality, please suggest that they read a good book or do some sort of creative work quietly. Secondly, when these particular students do not take their final exams, this gives you the opportunity to have less work to complete, which is always a nice side benefit.

If teachers are obligated to administer final exams to students, please give a guideline of how the final exam is. They may be given some possible questions so that they can prepare in advance. They may be assigned as homework some questions to develop, and there can be a discussion of these questions. It would be best for them and for you to take good notes at that time so that you can select which of those questions would be on their final exam.

One interesting approach to final exams is the following, which could be used in science classes, for example. There are different stations or areas in the classroom that the students have to rotate to in order to answer the questions with their own final exam papers. They are not permitted to look at someone else's final exam or to confer with anybody. You would circulate throughout the classroom to monitor their progress and to make sure that everybody is doing their own work. Upon completion of going through these different stations or areas in the classroom, they turn in their final exams.

Since you might be inundated with correcting final exams, it would be worth your while to give multiple choice questions with different possible answers. When having questions that have multiple possible answers, please consider indicating to the class as well that in the multiple choice portion of the final exam, that there will be instances in which they will have to mark two or more answers. If they were to mark only one answer and if there are several correct answers, then that response to that question would be incorrect. The reason for doing this is that students need to read each question along with all of the possible answers thoroughly.

How about imagining taking a final exam yourself that represents a major part of the class's grade? If a final exam is completely serious, it can place that much more stress on the students. By adding humorous answers that are completely incorrect, this can calm any fears and lighten the stress of the final exam. In fact, students may actually want to take your final exams as a result.

While multiple choice exams are a good way to determine how much they know, it is still a passive way to recall information. Please also include short and/or long written responses so that they need to think actively. It does not have to be extensive, but just enough so that you know what they have learned.

It is important to judge for yourself how long each final exam will take to correct along with tabulating and determining semester grades. This is important because time will be of the essence in terms of turning in your semester grades to the administration.

If you teach English, please think how much information is to be covered and how much time it will take to correct each final exam, seeing that there will not be too much time prior to having to turn in your grades. You may want to include an essay for them to write, but please be sure that it is not too long due to the fact that you need to correct all of their work in a timely fashion.

If a lengthy essay for part of their final exam is required and if permitted by the administration, what about allowing them to take a class period or two prior to the final exam to write their essays? Then there could be more time to read and to correct these essays. For the day of the final exam, perhaps multiple choice and/or short answers could be included.

Idea Number Twenty-Nine

Even though so much needs to be accomplished each day, you will be usually very accurate. Nevertheless, mistakes can be made in terms of the correcting of student work or reacting to certain situations in the classroom. When it comes to those times when you have made mistakes, please apologize to the students involved. The end result of revealing to your students that mistakes can happen can actually be very helpful because honesty is being demonstrated and students will probably behave more honestly. It can also result in more respect for all concerned.

Idea Number Thirty

There will be times when seniors in high school will be applying for such things as scholarships, grants, and/or loans and applying to different colleges and universities, for example. In turn, they will be requesting that teachers write letters of recommendation. The assumption may be that the teachers will write how well they have done in their classes. It needs to be remembered that letters of recommendation must be an accurate account of the achievements, the attitude, and the behavior of the students. Thus, it needs to be realistic because that is what these organizations, colleges, and universities wish to know and to judge.

Should you decide to write an outstanding letter of recommendation of the student, fine. Should you prefer not to write a letter of recommendation, it is best to tactfully suggest that he or she consider asking another teacher by saying that you are busy, for example. If the student has been misbehaving, immature, and sincerely not worthy of the honor for which he or she is applying, it is inappropriate to write such letters of recommendation. In this way, there is no confrontation. In actuality, there truly may be another teacher who has had better results with him or her.

The above ideas can be beneficial for your students so that learning is enhanced and so that discipline problems can decrease. Of course, individual students will react differently, but generally speaking, the results will prove to be more positive for all concerned.

Lastly, please experiment by doing something "outside the box" when there is a problem presented in terms of your students and their learning. Discussion of your ideas with your fellow teachers, with your family, and/or with your friends can be very beneficial. Also, please allow yourself time to ponder what needs to be done. The answers to your questions and to your concerns will eventually arise.

When you have discussed and determined what needs to be done, please try your ideas. If they work, congratulations. Success has been achieved. If they do not work, it is a way to determine what has not worked, but the answers will come eventually. Under these circumstances, please do not give up because you want to be even more effective as their teacher. The challenge may be presented, but patience to determine the solution will be helpful for a more positive experience for all concerned in your classroom environment.

~

CHAPTER TWENTY-THREE

Connecting the Classroom with the Outside World

Based on department budgets and possible time constraints, please consider having the world outside the school environment be part of the classroom as much as possible. The more that students are able to link your subject with the "real world," the more students will value its importance. They are more apt to see why they need to focus without being a discipline problem as well, if they are prone to being that way. If they are conscientious, it will solidify and support what is being studied in the classroom.

Many high schools lately have changed their educational goals by focusing on vocational education. Even if they are not, many students are allowed to get training of a particular field at vocational schools.

If and when there are field trips, please consider preparing a set of questions for your students so that field trips have a purpose. They will then be keenly aware as to specific details about the job sites and about the persons that will be visited. Thus, it is not simply a day off.

Here are some "real world" possibilities for consideration, if you have not chosen to do these types of activities already.

If available, English and drama classes may want to consider attending Renaissance fairs and to wear clothes of that time period. You may want to attend plays with your class. Writers and/or actors and actresses can be invited to attend class to give presentations about literature being studied and/or take questions from students.

Art classes can go to art museums to have a guided tour from docents, and/or you may require that they go there on a regular basis to view and to find out about exhibited paintings. In turn, they would need to do research projects based on your criteria. Students can go to a natural setting or to a busy section of your town or city so that they can draw what they see. Artists can be invited to attend class so that the students can learn different techniques of drawing and understand what the business aspects are for having art as a primary or a secondary job.

Photography classes can go to different parts of the city and to different parts of the countryside to take photos. Arrangements can be made to visit photography studios to see how photographers deal with lighting and people. Newspaper reporters and photographers can be invited to your classes to allow students to ask questions about what it means to explore news stories from their points of view.

Business and economics classes can go to companies to find out how they function and to ask questions of employees and/or the bosses there. Speakers from companies can be invited to your classroom in order to discuss what it is like to work in such settings and what it means to be responsible. You could invite self-employed people to speak about their jobs and their opportunities.

Agriculture classes can take field trips to cattle ranches to see what it is like to have to take care of these animals twenty-four hours a day, seven days a week, besides the normal amount of students tending to animals during the school week. You may want to invite business classes to attend so that both the agriculture and business classes learn what it means to help feed the general public locally, statewide, nationally, and possibly internationally along with the financial implications involved. You can take your students to county, state, and national fairs that have agricultural focuses and competitions.

For family living and/or psychology classes, perhaps your students could go to a homeless family shelter so that everyone interacts with people whom they normally do not meet. Perhaps some toys, food, drinks, and clothing that the students have opted to get rid of could be brought as well. Perhaps a local counselor could be invited to discuss with classes what it means to be more mature, to have more responsibilities by getting a job, to have a more emotionally satisfying life, and to have quality time with family, if they are so inclined.

Home economics classes can take field trips to local cafés, restaurants, and bed-and-breakfast establishments to see what it is like to work there. Cooks can be invited to attend classes to show how to prepare their special meals. Perhaps they can discuss what it means to have food ingredients be shipped in a timely fashion to their establishments. These types of speakers would be ideal to discuss what it means to eat and to drink healthy items for a better life physically.

Physics classes can go to nearby amusement parks in order to analyze different rides from a scientific perspective. Physicists can be invited to the classroom in order to explain some practical applications to their daily lives.

Math classes can go to a grassy area of the high school campus. In pairs, one student can hurl an object while the other student measures the distance. Afterward, the students can reverse their responsibilities, and they can determine who threw the object the farthest and also determine how to calculate in different forms of measuring: for example, the metric system. This can be done a variety of times to determine the averages. Mathematicians can be invited to the classroom to have them explain the relevance of their jobs and how mathematics is important to students in their daily lives.

Foreign language classes can attend multicultural events in the community in order to get that much more of an appreciation of the studied culture along with possibly attending other events of other cultures not studied. A dance instructor can be invited to show students how to dance different dances of your foreign language's country. People of those cultures who have immigrated to the United States can possibly be invited in order to give their perspectives about their native countries and about the United States.

Here are some ideas for those students who are considered minorities at your school. An activity worthy of consideration is to have students of foreign descent and Caucasian students take field trips together to learn more about one another and to break down any prejudices that each group may have of one another. You can invite foreign exchange students at your school to describe their native countries. Of particular interest may be those students whose families have fled war-torn countries or those students whose families left their countries in hope of a better economic life in this country.

If you teach Spanish and/or another language that is prevalent in your town or city, there may be health fairs for those individuals and families who may not have insurance. Students may be interested in attending health fairs so that they can speak their target language being learned but also to be a support system for families waiting in lines.

Social studies classes can take field trips to local government offices in order to interview local officials to find out what it is like to govern your area. Field trips to historical museums that pertain to your subject can be beneficial. Inviting potential candidates for a political debate into your class could be very enlightening. Current political leaders can be invited to discuss their points of view about society. You can utilize www.earth.google.com to locate different sites around the world as they pertain to your subject matter.

Physical education classes can take field trips to sporting events in the community and to allow the students to listen to coaches and/or players discussing their sports. It might be interesting for these sports figures to discuss their importance to the public and to discuss their views on such topics as dedication and steroids.

Special education classes can take field trips to local businesses to see how businesses are run. In this way, they can become that much more inspired by what they see, and they may want to pursue a career in business.

ROTC classes can take field trips to boot camps on bases so that the students learn survival skills. You could also have current and/or retired military personnel attend your classes to have them explain what it means to participate in the military. If they have participated in wars, they may want to discuss what it means to fight for survival and for specific causes. It may be also interesting for them to discuss what it means to return from fighting in terms of how they have been able to adjust to a calmer style of living.

Drafting classes can take field trips to visit local buildings and bridges to analyze these structures. You can also invite civil engineers to your class to discuss the benefits of their field of work and to have the students ask questions.

If available at your high school, another vital resource is the Career Guidance Center, whose counselor-in-charge has different speakers discussing career options. They may also be able to provide the possibility of employment and high school credit for students.

A side benefit of involving students in field trips and having guest speakers from the community is that it shows businesses that the school system is interested in real-life experiences, thus creating a better bond between all concerned.

CHAPTER TWENTY-FOUR

~

Coaching a Sport

If you are a coach, there is so much more to coaching a sport than just telling your athletes what to do on the playing field, as you well know.

Your knowledge and appreciation of that sport more than likely were the reasons you became involved in it. You may be or may wish to become an assistant coach or a head coach. Perhaps being an assistant coach is preferable so that there may be less stress. Being the head coach may be considered a gigantic, yet prestigious position, but seeing that there may be a head coach already, you may need to settle to be an assistant coach, at least for now.

Whichever status you may have as a coach, please consider the following suggestions. Some are rather well known already, while some others may be understood but need to be noted.

Nowadays, finances are a critical factor and a possible concern. There may be a minmal amount of financial support to have a healthy, vibrant program with convenient bus transportation, enough uniforms, and functional equipment. Parents or guardians and their young adults may have to pay for a variety of items. Having a parent boosters' program can truly help by selling food and drinks at games with the profits going to the athletic program. There may be annual fund-raising events, like wine tasting events, dances, and auctions, for example.

While parent or guardian support for their young adults in athletic programs can be beneficial, it can also create problems for coaches. While parents or guardians try to be objective, they truly have one goal. They want their young adults playing as much as humanly possible. Thus, they can become either very supportive of your program when they are participating or very argumentative of your program.

The supportive parents or guardians will be pleased when their young adults play, but if they do not play at a particular time due to another player having more ability, they can be very understanding. These supportive adults can appreciate your desire of team building and team effort in order to do the best possible job in the sport.

Nevertheless, coaches will probably be confronted with very argumentative parents or guardians when their young adults are "sidelined," which can result in them becoming very defensive, stating that you are being unfair or playing "favorites," for example.

In order to potentially prevent such confrontations, it is important to have meetings with parents or guardians and potential players prior to the season of the sport. At that time, coaches can state their expectations of players, including that these young adults need to condition themselves well during the off-season for maximum results. It does not mean they will automatically play every minute of every game. In this way, any tension between the coaches, the players, and their parents or guardians can be lessened.

Next, it is to your advantage to stress the importance of good conduct and good sportsmanship at all games by not only the players but also the parents or guardians because many school districts and counties have strict rules as to what is acceptable and unacceptable behavior with the appropriate consequences. Also, coaches might consider saying that adults need to be role models for their young adults and should enjoy the game experience without shouting rude remarks. After all, coaches and referees are trained in the sport while the audience does not necessarily have the same expertise.

When there are meetings with the potential players, coaches can find out about their history playing the sport, their skills, and which positions they have played previously, if they are not known already. Then, the coaches usually meet to determine potential players and which positions they would be best suited for playing. Rotating their playing spots can help to determine which position is not only best for them specifically, but also what is best for the entire team's potential success, which is the ultimate goal for coaches.

At this meeting, emphasis needs to be stressed that student athletes need to do the best they can in this sport when competing against other schools. Also, there can be plenty of times when the team will win. Learning how to win with humility is important. They certainly will deserve praise for all of their hard work.

While not the most pleasant thing to think about, there can be plenty of times when the team may lose. Yes, that can be an emotional letdown for the coaches and for the players. Coaches thus need to act with tact, which may be difficult to practice since there can be frustrations about how they were playing.

Learning how to lose with the students' heads high is important so that they can learn from this experience in order to make fewer mistakes in the future. Indeed, losing can be a gift. Under these circumstances, it is best to accentuate the positive qualities of what they did well and also to point out where they could have done better. Of course, this is easier said than done, but it ultimately can translate into better self-esteem, accepting responsibility, and better performance in the next games.

Please emphasize good eating and good drinking habits by the players all the time. Since coaches are their role models, it is best to suggest which foods are healthy for them and which foods should be disregarded. Eating candy may be sweet, but it is detrimental for their performance and for their overall health. Drinking a lot of water instead of sodas and power-boosting drinks is very helpful during practices and games. Lastly, special discussion needs to take place in regard to the bad consequences of steroids physically and emotionally, school punishments, and how they can be affected when they are adults.

Since participation in a sport does take time, practice, and teamwork, please emphasize to the students that they are expected to do their best to participate in all practices. After all, playing a sport is a commitment that they have chosen to accept.

Time is an essential ingredient. Your players need to make the commitment to themselves, to the rest of the team, and to coaches in order to be there on time and for the full time of the practices. Of course, there can be situations beyond their control, but they should try to abide by certain rules as much as possible.

Practice means for them to follow the appropriate steps that will improve the chances that they will all succeed. One word of caution: please do not have them do an excessive amount of exercises because there have been instances of medical problems and even deaths by players.

Teamwork needs to be stressed because there is a better likelihood of success with team effort. Related to teamwork, there will be times when your team will feel so energized that they may want to do something together. Players may want to shave their heads or wear insignias showing cooperation among the players just for the fun of it and/or to show support of a student who has medical problems, for example. Please encourage this type of behavior as long as it is appropriate and an inspiration for the overall team and for the cause.

In terms of players misbehaving inside and/or outside the classroom, there are strict guidelines to adhere to. By stressing the fact that playing a sport is a privilege and not a right, coaches are supporting the other teachers for appropriate behavior in the entire school community.

If coaches hear about misbehavior by the players in the classroom, it is essential to talk with the players involved. If the players have broken a school rule, they need to be sidelined or removed from the team, depending upon the severity of the misbehavior. Of course, depending upon the degree of the infraction, the school's rules take precedence, and the students may need to suffer the consequences of their actions, like detention, suspension, or even expulsion.

Please always accentuate the fact to your players that they have very good abilities and that they need to not have a superiority complex. They are representatives of their school. They are participating to play for their school. They need to be positive role models for the students who do not play their sport or any sport. When they start bossing others around because they believe they are better than anyone else, coaches need to have a stern in-your-face discussion with them to eliminate this attitude.

Depending upon the individual players, there may be students who do not do well academically but achieve a lot of success in your sport. There are typically specific guidelines in terms of academic achievement. Oftentimes, counties will have athletic organizations and/or school districts that require a minimum of a 2.0 GPA (grade point average).

In order to make sure that they are doing acceptable work in their classes, high schools can require grade checks that they take to each of their teachers to determine grades along with any appropriate comments. This is good for coaches, for players, for their parents or guardians, and for the administration.

In order to hopefully improve the chances that players attain that minimum GPA, coaches oftentimes may have specific study sessions for the students between the conclusion of their classes and the start of their workouts in which they work on their homework and study for quizzes and tests. There may not be any time between the time school concludes and when they can reasonably begin practicing, which necessitates the emphasis to the student athletes that they must organize their time accordingly in order to complete all of their work and studying for the next school day after returning home.

Some students will meet the minimum GPA just to be involved in their favorite sport in school. Thus, any way that coaches can encourage students with academic issues will certainly help not only the other players but ultimately their future. Perhaps if there would be student athletes who have the same classes together, you could suggest that they work together as much as possible.

For the fun of it and with the permission of the players and the administration, you might want to consider having your players perform a comical sports presentation or skit at school rallies. This will show the amusing side of players and promote the school's attendance at games.

Toward the end of the season of this sport, coaches normally will determine a way to recognize achievement by players. That can consist of an awards dinner with the players and parents or guardians attending. That can be a recognition of players at a sports rally at school. Highlighting all players is exceptionally important so that everyone is recognized and encouraged for future years in high school and possibly for college or the university level, if they are so inclined.

Your role as a sports coach can truly enrich your players and their future because there will be times when university and college coaches may wish to observe them in action. It is best to accentuate their strengths along with indicating where they still might need some work.

Also, as was suggested in a previous chapter, players may ask for letters of recommendation. If you believe they are worthy of the letters of recommendation, great. If you prefer not to do so, it is best to be tactful and say that they need to work harder in order for a very good letter of recommendation to be written. Bottom line, the players know if they are worthy of a positive or a not so positive letter.

All of your efforts for helping players to become responsible are very commendable. Indeed, coaching does take a lot of time, practice, encouragement, and praise of student athletes both in the sport as well as in their regular studies. It does take a lot of tact to improve any concerns. It also does take a lot of cooperation by both the student athletes and their parents. Thank you for your extra dedication above and beyond your normal teaching responsibilities!

~

CHAPTER TWENTY-FIVE

Coaching the Academic Decathlon

There are many elementary schools whose teachers and students participate in spelling bees, the Science Olympiad, and the Academic Pentathlon. These are fabulous academic competitions so that students learn how to expand their knowledge, learn how to work with other students, and compete against other schools in their counties. These students oftentimes will thrive on competition, and once they attend high school, they will probably participate in speech competitions and debate competitions, all to prepare themselves oftentimes for the challenges of the Academic Decathlon. It is strange that the Academic Decathlon usually does not have the highest regard of the entire school community, but it is an exceptional, inspiring experience.

If you think of your most challenging subject in college or at the university and multiply that by ten, that is how each subject of the Academic Decathlon can be. It truly does take nearly a full year of collaborative work with students, the coach or ideally the coaches, and perhaps other adults who are experts of their field that the students will be studying.

The Academic Decathlon consists of studying mathematics of every kind and various studies in the fields of science, world history, art and art history, economics, language and literature, and music, and the tests for these subjects are usually multiple choice without the public being present. The students need to prepare an organized speech of three and a half to four minutes. They also have an impromptu speech of one and a half to two minutes. They lastly are interviewed.

The team consists of three A students, three B students, and three C students. If a teacher looks through student transcripts, there will normally be the overall GPA including every class and the academic overall GPA, which is the one that is needed for the Academic Decathlon potential candidates.

A student may be moved from the C level to the B or A level, if desired, but a student may not be moved from the A level to the B or C level. If it is believed a C or a B student will excel on a higher level, fine. Nevertheless, please adjust the composition of the team so that there are ideally three students at each level.

After reviewing student transcripts, it might also be a good idea to confer with their teachers or to distribute to them a questionnaire. In this way, the strengths and the potential drawbacks of each of the students can be determined. Then those students who are believed to be the best candidates could be invited to a special meeting in order to introduce the concept of the Academic Decathlon. Of course, having students who stand out remarkably well in your own classes can be considered as well, and there may have been students in the previous year who wish to continue with the Academic Decathlon experience.

Another possible way to include students is to announce in the daily bulletin announcement and to put up posters in school about a meeting of potential Academic Decathlon students and then promoting the benefits of being involved in this effort. The benefits include expanding their knowledge beyond their classes, working with other students of their own caliber, earning high school credit if possible, competing against other high schools locally and possibly on the state and national levels, earning recognition from their classmates, possibly earning scholarships from universities, and having this academic activity look good for their applications for scholarships, colleges, and universities.

Also, please take note of these considerations for the team. The best students can be academically inclined, but if they wish to rely strictly on their academic history and to do very little for the team, that is an indicator as to possibly not wanting to devote much time and energy to this cause. They need to devote extra time and extra effort in order to achieve any form of success for the team. Thus, if there are any students who become lazy, please advise them that they need to focus better or they will be replaced by other students.

Another aspect of students to consider is how busy they are with their classes, with sports, with clubs and organizations, and possibly with work. It is important not to overburden students, even though they might have the best intentions of wanting to become team members.

Should you not have a complete team of nine students due to any number of reasons, please still consider participating in the Academic Decathlon. Nevertheless, any team with less than nine cannot possibly win the overall competition because all nine scores are combined in order to determine the overall winner.

Along with the main team of nine students, there can be as many alternates as you wish who can consist of any grade on the high school level, but it is mostly desirable to include those students who are freshmen and sophomores, although some juniors can be included. In this way, these students will gain the experience of this competition with the possiblity of being a part of the actual team of nine for the competition the following school year, if they choose to participate then. The alternates too can participate in the multiple choice tests, but they do not compete in the speech competitions, the interview competitions, nor in the Super Quiz.

Generally speaking, please consider your junior and senior students for the Academic Decathlon team because these particular students are generally that much more mature, that much more confident, and that much more knowledgeable than freshmen and sophomores. Of course, there are freshmen and sophomores who are very gifted and very mature that may be able to handle themselves very well for such a study and competition.

Prior to the competition or on the day or days of the competition, students write an essay based on one of three prompts offered, which can typically be a general quote that the students can relate to, a question related to current events, and also a question pertaining to a part of the literature being studied for the Academic Decathlon competition. They are usually given an hour to complete this essay, and this part of the competition is monitored.

The students also need to prepare for the Super Quiz topic, which is usually the overall theme of the studies of the competition. In contrast to the multiple choice tests, which are individually taken, there are individual students who answer the multiple choice questions literally within a matter of seconds after it is being read to them. Indeed, the Super Quiz portion of the competition is probably one of the most stressful parts of the competition due to the fact that the general public is invited to attend this event in an auditorium.

In preparation for this event, there is usually at least one meeting that can take place at the county level for Academic Decathlon coaches at the beginning of the school year in order to gain information about how the county's Academic Decathlon functions and what responsibilities coaches have. They can meet other Academic Decathlon coaches from different high schools, and they might learn what has worked and what has not worked for them, although they typically will not disclose any or many techniques that they use for successful competitions. After all, one does not usually give advice to one's competitors.

The Academic Decathlon may or may not be offered at your high school because it does require money for this class or these classes, books, possible field trips, and substitute teachers at times. Also, there may be other required classes that may take precedent. If it is a part of your standard school day, which is the ideal situation, there is the additional pressure to make sure that there are enough students in this class every year so that the administration will approve the existence of this class.

With cutbacks in education as of late, the Academic Decathlon may be considered as an elective class, thus necessitating the elimination of the class oftentimes and having it become an extracurricular class instead, if available at all. If so, students and coaches need to meet before or after school, during weekends, and during vacations.

An Academic Decathlon coach will generally have few, if any, complaints from these students' parents or guardians because they will usually support their young adults' expansion of their knowledge.

It is suggested to review the topics in detail based on the outline supplied as to what the students are expected to know and to determine different ideas that will enliven the material for students.

During the year, which oftentimes can be during part of the summer as well, you need to work with your students, any teachers who wish to help out, and any outside community members who may wish to help out. There may be willing teachers and willing community members who would like to give details about the specific areas of study because these individuals are already enthusiastic about the material, which can translate into inspiring students that much more. Also, these adults may like to deal with students who are really eager to learn without being discipline problems, generally speaking.

Another way to help students understand the material better is for them to select and to do their research work on a specific area that they are interested in. Since they may have shown an interest in a particular area, in turn, they may become that much more enthusiastic. After doing the research work, you would request that they present the information at specific times of the year to the other students who would take extensive notes.

Perhaps you could consider having a combination of yourself with your subject matter, willing teachers with their subject matter, willing community members with their subject matter, and student presentations so that all the students would become that much more prepared for the Academic Decathlon competition.

As for the organized speech, the impromptu portion, and the interview, if you are a drama or speech teacher, you can help your students rather easily. If not, it is advisable to have your students work with Toastmasters, which is a group of adults well trained to help students to be able to speak better in front of others. If you go to www.toastmasters.org, a club probably can be found in your area.

Requiring them to maintain a notebook to collect and to review all notes can be very helpful. If you are lucky enough to have this class as part of the normal school day, you also need to record grades just like any other class.

If going on field trips is possible, please organize them in a way that they include a full day, whether it means going to art and science museums and/or interviewing people pertaining to the subjects that need to be studied in depth.

If finances are a major concern in order to go on field trips or have speakers and/or extra materials, it is suggested to have any type of fund-raising event possible and to perhaps seek donations from parents, guardians, and any community group that supports education. Also, seeking donations from the school site council and from the local PTSA chapter would be other possible resources to consider.

If the Academic Decathlon is an extracurricular activity, please consider giving them credits toward their graduation and thus having them earn grades. Considering that they are studying so many subjects with so much depth, if the administration agrees, it is a good idea to have your students earn a minimum of double the amount of credits that are earned in a typical class for the year. After all, they are completing a lot of work, which deserves recognition and can be helpful for applying to colleges and universities along with applying for scholarships, grants, and loans.

If this is considered an extracurricular activity, please consider determining grades by their regular attendance, their work as a team member, their work that they turn in to you (essays and notes, for example), their organized and impromptu speeches, and their attendance at the competition itself.

When the competition approaches, please have your students take one or several days off from school with you so that all can review whatever is needed to review. These review sessions on campus could be in your library or, as was already mentioned in a previous chapter, at a mountain retreat, if it is permitted and financially possible.

These review sessions need to consist of an organized review by you with questions and answers. Perhaps it could be a fun activity by making it a friendly competition. Also, please allow them to work either individually or in pairs part of the time because they know their own strengths and the areas they need to devote more time to reviewing. Lastly, they need to rehearse their organized speeches and to practice impromptu speaking along with how to interview well. This could be done in front of the other decathletes and/or in front of adults, like teachers who wish to help them and/or adults in the community.

In order to involve the entire high school, please consider making announcements over the intercom about the Academic Decathlon event with the date and the time. Also, if there is a rally, that can generate that much more support and enthusiasm for the team, possibly leading to students attending the public session of the competition and to even more students participating in the Academic Decathlon in the future.

For the day of the Academic Decathlon competition, it is best to establish a phone tree in which students are notified to get up in time so that they meet at a place that you determine. If parents or guardians are able to volunteer to drive students to the competition and to return them, that is the ideal. If not, depending upon how many students are on your entire team, a school van or bus may be needed, although there are charges that the school district will require.

Please ask your students to dress in attire that looks respectable and that they would wear for interview purposes. If they have no concept as to what that means, please explain to them what that means. Boys should wear a tie, a white shirt, dark pants, shined shoes, and a nice sweater, a sports coat outfit with a tie, or a suit. Their shirts need to be tucked in as well. Girls should wear dresses, but not high heels. Students are trying to make a favorable impression to the speech and interview judges along with making a favorable impression of their school. They should not wear any insignias or emblems that refer to their high school because if the judges have any prejudices about the high school, it may be reflected in the overall score of the speeches. That normally does not happen, but it may.

The Academic Decathlon competition is either one or several days during the school year. It will begin usually early in the morning and will last typically until the late afternoon. There are breaks during the day for snacks along with drinks and for lunch, which normally need to be supplied by the coaches. So please determine the times and the locations for these breaks so that you and possibly the parents or guardians can provide food and drinks available for them. At the end of the competition the awards' presentation will take place, thus completing the county Academic Decathlon competition.

After all the studying, preparation, possible field trips, and time, it is suggested to remind the students that they will have all won by learning the information during the year and by working together. It will have been a great experience for all concerned. They also will have learned from the Academic Decathlon experience that they can achieve success with time and work on everybody's part when working as a team.

The winning school on the county level consists of only the main team of nine students, and they can earn individual and school awards. The alternates, the students who do not participate in the speeches and the Super Quiz, win only individual awards at the county level, and they do not compete in subsequent competitions.

After the competition is finished on the county level, the winning team of nine students only will advance to the state competition level, which can last several days. The teams on the state level are thus the winners of each county. The team that wins on the state level will advance to the national championship, which also can last several days.

Whether you are an athletic coach or an Academic Decathlon coach, you are to be congratulated for all of your efforts with your students. You truly will be making an everlasting impression upon your students, and you will certainly be a major highlight of their high school experiences. They will understand the importance of being responsible for themselves, being dependent upon others, team building, and dedication.

It may be a good idea to invite the student competitors and the parents or guardians to attend a casual meal and awards presentation and to recognize all of them for their support.

CHAPTER TWENTY-SIX

~

If and When You Still Have Extra Time and Extra Energy

Since you can be inundated with your teaching responsibilities, especially during the first five years, it is advisable to focus all of your professional time and attention to perfecting your teaching, including lesson plans, different methods of instruction, worksheets, quizzes, tests, projects, and disciplinary procedures for your students. After approximately five years, you may wish to consider extending your professional responsibilities, if desired and if and when you have extra time and extra energy to do so. Of course, if the administration assigns you to work on school committees, it is necessary to fulfill those obligations.

This suggestion may apply to those teachers who have had teaching experience to a certain extent if they have transferred to a new high school. Since they are more experienced but new to the high school, it may take only one or two years instead of a completely new teacher who should wait for approximately five years.

One way to create more of a bond between yourself and your students is to possibly attend student functions. Of course, if the administration requires teachers to sign up for these types of activities for chaperoning purposes, that is what needs to be done.

No matter what will be the reason for attending student functions, it is a great opportunity to show you care for them as human beings and what they do outside the realm of the classroom environment. Perhaps answering any questions that they might pose in regard to your class can be helpful for them and for you to ask them about their perception of the class so far.

Above all else, it is an opportunity to become more acquainted with high school students.

When students have club car washes outside the school day (typically on a Saturday) and if your car might need a car wash, please consider supporting them by getting your car washed and donating money to their cause.

You could be involved with different committees for the advancement of the school and the students, like the school site council or the high school's PTSA.

Student-teachers are full of energy. They are ready to learn, and just as importantly, they are ready to teach. With at least five years of teaching experience, having already established certain teaching techniques that can be a benefit for your students, you are thus able to exhibit realistic confidence and guidance to student-teachers. They can learn while still being able to develop their own style of teaching.

Also, even though student-teachers have learned the theoretical development of teaching and learning styles, they definitely need to observe students in actual classrooms. They need to determine what discipline style they feel most comfortable with. They need to learn how to develop realistic lesson plans that can be beneficial for all of their students.

It is vitally important that there is a discussion about your grading procedures so that there is consistency in terms of what the student-teachers do when they take over your class completely.

To keep the lines of communication open, it is desirable for you and your student-teachers to exchange phone numbers and e-mail addresses.

Student-teachers need to follow the guidelines requested by their administrator-in-charge. You too will need to adhere to the guidelines for working with student-teachers.

When the administrator-in-charge for student-teachers, the student-teachers, and you decide that it is appropriate, the student-teachers need to be in charge of the class or the classes. It is important for you to stay in the classroom because the administrator-in-charge wants you to give appropriate feedback upon completion of each class. The time frame for you remaining as an observer in the classroom needs to be determined by the administrator-in-charge. Once that specific period of time has concluded, please be sure to confer with your student-teachers daily in order to be their support system.

Depending upon how long you have been teaching and how you relate to other teachers, the administration, and the rest of the school community, you could possibly earn the right to become a mentor teacher to new teachers, if there would be a mentor-type program available in your school district. It would be best to think about why you are interested in becoming a mentor because the interview team typically consists of teachers and administrators who will be asking questions related to the mentor position.

It is important to check with the high school and/or district for the appropriate procedures for applying and becoming a mentor teacher. Since there are other teachers who also qualify, there may be a lot of competition.

Upon applying to become a mentor, it is important for you to dress very nicely because it is an interview for a job. Prior to entering the room, please be sure to take a big, deep breath in order to calm yourself. This will help you relax and be able to thoughtfully respond to their questions. The interviewing team may consist of a minimum of six school district employees, typically some teachers and administrators whom you know and some whom you do not know. Before answering their questions, please be sure to think for a moment as to what has been requested. Then please answer succinctly and consider the benefits of how you can help new teachers to become better engaged with their students.

Should the interviewing team select someone else, there is always next time. The interviewing process will then feel that much more comfortable, and your answers may be phrased more succinctly. Also, by having extra time until the next interviewing session, this will give you an opportunity to help out more teachers and to become that much more involved in the school process, all of which translates into more experience and a better chance to convince the interviewing team of your qualifications to become a mentor teacher.

Upon being selected as a mentor teacher, congratulations! You deserve the honor. You can help new teachers to gain the confidence and the expertise to achieve the same success that you have already attained. Since the attrition rate for new teachers can be quite high, anything a mentor teacher can do to help them will be greatly appreciated by the administration, fellow teachers, students, and parents or guardians. It is also quite rewarding to help them relieve their stress along with their frustrations and to be their guide on the side.

One of the most challenging and rewarding experiences in order to help an entire high school is accreditation, the evaluation process that usually takes place every six years by outside teams, consisting of administrators, teachers, and sometimes students and parents or guardians. It is a lengthy process that does require a lot of teamwork and cooperation by the entire school community: administrators, teachers, counselors, school psychologists, specialists, classified staff, students, and parents or guardians. It is a way to determine the strengths and the areas of improvement for the school, and the final assessment by the team will be how long the school is recognized by your state.

Teachers will be assigned to at least one group because they are an integral part of the school community. Should you have any extra time, the administration probably would appreciate any extra help. Also, it shows the administration that you care enough to want to participate in this process. It does require more time and more energy on your part. Yet, that much more will be learned about working with others and ultimately in helping the high school improve that much more.

While being a member of an accreditation committee means doing one's best in support of it, you may be asked to become the chairperson of a committee, which has more obligations. This would mean that you would need to make sure that everyone in that committee is cooperating by fulfilling specific duties for the successful completion of the overall report. It can be a very enlightening experience to learn more, to validate the school's goal of teaching today's youth, and to determine where the high school needs to improve.

If you are asked and if you agree to become the accreditation chairperson for the entire school, if there is any way that your administration will allow it to become a reality, they may even give you a period off so that the best possible job can be done. If you are not able to have a period off for the accreditation process due to the fact that there is a need for you to teach your classes, it is a good idea to request to have an assistant accreditation chairperson so that the two of you can divide the responsibilities to complete this process thoroughly. Also, it will require a lot of organization and attendance at many meetings with different groups.

Please consider talking with the counselors to see if there might be one or ideally two students who wish to become teacher assistants. They can help with the organization of this accreditation process with your direction.

After having participated in the accreditation process at the local high school level, there may be time to participate in an accreditation team evaluating other high schools. You need to get the permission from your school site administration first before proceeding with this idea and from the central accreditation office by following their guidelines. Please note that attendance of a workshop that deals with the accreditation process will be required prior to the beginning of the evaluation process of a school.

Once you have been notified about which school is to be evaluated, the accreditation chairperson will send you the entire school's accreditation report. He or she will assign several areas and/or departments to read and to analyze according to specific standards that will have already been learned in the workshop. The other members of the accreditation will be assigned the other sections.

In preparation for the visitation to the assigned school, you need to fill out the regular paperwork to have a substitute teacher. Also, lesson plans will need to be specific for your substitute teacher because the visitation is typically three and a half days.

The visitation is rewarding, oftentimes intense work from early in the morning until sometimes late at night. You will be requested to observe classes and to attend committee meetings. It will require talking with your fellow accreditation team members to determine the validity of their report.

This process is a way to help another high school to help themselves. In addition, new perspectives about high school education are learned, and you may even want to share some of these learned ideas with your high school administration or even to implement them in the classroom.

Depending upon your school district, there may be a process to nominate and to select the high school teacher of the year along with the elementary school teacher of the year. When you have taught for many years in one specific school district, then you may be encouraged to apply or to initiate the nomination. Like the mentor nomination process, there may be times in which you may be accepted. If so, congratulations! If you are not selected, just to be considered and to go through the process can be quite an honor and something to be learned from in order to possibly earn that privilege the next time.

In your district, you could be involved with the local teachers' union in order to support teachers. It provides a great service for the district's teachers, and it can require a lot of work and time away from the classroom. There are state and national teachers' organizations in which you can participate as well, if you so desire.

You could be part of district committees for the improvement of the entire district. While it could mean taking time off from classes, you could be an integral part of your district's educational program for the benefit of the students ultimately.

For any of the above activities and/or for any other activities that take place at your high school in which you participate, please be sure to document them in your resume. Having such documentation can be helpful for possible awards and advancement.

You may want to consider taking classes in order to increase your salary and to earn an advanced degree for salary advancement or possibly an administrative credential. If so, please try not to inundate yourself with so much additional work outside the classroom because you may become less effective in what is being taught.

All of the above ideas should be considered if and when you still have extra time and extra energy. These activities and many more will ultimately help students in their pursuit of a great education. Thus, please be selective as to which activities you wish to pursue because the reason you are employed for that high school is to teach your students as fully and as effectively as possible with few distractions.

~

CHAPTER TWENTY-SEVEN

"You Can Make More Tomorrows Than a Person Can Possibly Count"

—Miklos Fejer

You are an extremely important individual who needs to actively be aware of what you personally need. Your energy level can be maintained by means of eating and drinking healthy things. Exercising on a regular basis will help you relieve stress, maintain your energy, and live life in a healthy fashion. Sleeping well can help you restore your energy level for your regular responsibilities. So anything that ultimately helps is to be encouraged and to be consistently practiced. In turn, you will have the ability to help others, including your family, friends, and the school community.

Teaching is a wonderful profession. It certainly does require a lot of planning and effort to accomplish learning by the students. It requires a lot of empathy and understanding of one's students and their potential. It requires mutual respect. It requires a lot of genuine encouragement for those students who struggle in their classes. It requires a lot of genuine praise when they have done outstandingly well. It also requires having high expectations. It requires humor when appropriate. It requires creative and critical thinking. You have the ability to reach and to inspire your students academically and emotionally a majority of the time. Also, the family unit needs hope so that all of them will work in unison and so that the young adults will have a better opportunity of succeeding in their classes.

While the above goals are lofty and achievable, teachers need to remember that there is always room for improvement. Nobody is a perfect teacher. Everybody can become a better teacher. As a matter of fact, so-called mistakes are gifts in that while there may be disappointments due to discipline issues, academic issues, and sometimes during competitive events, they can be the beginning of better and more significant ways to improve your teaching ability and student learning.

Parents or guardians can be a teacher's best advocates in their homes so that their young adults can learn your subject matter better and so that students can become more cooperative in class. Parents or guardians can also be a major challenge in many respects by continuously criticizing what the teacher has done as has been related to them by their young adults, which is only getting one side of the situation.

Parents or guardians can also become and remain major critics of their own young adults, which is truly unfortunate, and these young adults will thus live down to the expectations of their parents or guardians magnificently and oftentimes rebel in their teenage years or during their entire lives. Thus, to hopefully make a positive impact on the parents or guardians, it is extremely important for the teacher to try to adjust their mindset so that they have a better, more positive perspective of their growing young adults.

Whenever discussing students with their parents or guardians, the teacher needs to accentuate the positive attributes of their young adults along with how there can be some notable improvement when their young adults apply themselves. This can be done by making specific suggestions, including extra help with them, specific ways to study, and anything else that is important for successful learning and for better cooperation.

Confidentiality between the teacher, students, and their parents or guardians is always important to maintain. When having discussions with a particular student and/or parents or guardians, they may wish to divulge certain information, which is fine and desirable in order to maintain trust between all concerned. Thus, it is advisable to guard information that pertains to a particular family and not to share it with other students and other parents and/or guardians. Of course, sharing it with school officials like other teachers and the administrative staff may be needed.

Yes, parents and guardians are essential ingredients of the happiness, the well-being, and the education of the young people whom they are trying to guide. That is why it is important to always have open communication with parents or guardians so that all of you can become a team, the advocates of the youth of today who will be adults and leaders of tomorrow.

The other extremely important factor in education will always be the students themselves. They may take delight in being in school or simply believe it is a waste of time from their perspective.

Whatever their attitude may be about school, they are accountable for their academic achievement and for their behavior. When they pay attention in class, they enhance their opportunities to learn. When they choose to be distracted, they are choosing to lose information, and their grades may consequently suffer. When they behave in class, they listen better and learn more. When they misbehave in class, they listen and learn less. When they cooperate at home by doing their work in a timely fashion, they understand more and will likely earn better grades. When they do not cooperate well at home due to being distracted or by being so tired continuously, their chances of learning become less. They quite possibly can be lost from that point on in their studies in your class. So teachers are like mirrors because they reflect what students do and what they don't do. All you can do is to do your best and hope for the best.

You relate more than simply the subject. You teach students to have high, realistic expectations and how to evolve and to transcend their perceived realities and limitations. Even the most reserved student has learned a lot about the subject and has also been empowered with the ability to improve as an individual. It is then the choice of the individual to either become inspired or to wait until later in his or her life in order to blossom into the individual with that much more personal and professional success.

To support and to understand your importance as a teacher, it would be a good idea to check www.teachermovie.com for a very heart warming video on this topic. Please also view the movie *Mr. Holland's Opus* with Richard Dreyfuss, even if you have already viewed it. These are movies that can live forever in the hearts and the minds of teachers and students!

It may be advantageous for you to keep in contact with some or many of your graduates personally, by means of www.classmates.com, www.facebook .com, or any other social network to see what path they have taken. You truly will be amazed at what they have done, and since the formality of teacher and student relationship will no longer exist, they are apt to share how significant an impact you have been for them.

When you do decide to retire, this is a serious and important decision to make. Please consider this question: What would you like to do upon retirement that you have not been able to do due to your professional responsibilities? As individual as you are will be all the possibilities.

Should you wish to still involve yourself as a teacher but not have the role on a regular basis, there is the option of becoming a substitute teacher. Then you have the option of consenting or declining to become a substitute teacher on any given day based on your personal plans. Students typically can test the substitute teacher; however, by being a substitute teacher in the high school where you have taught right after retirement, there will be more students who will know you. Of course, as the years pass by, it then may become more of a challenge since they will not know you, even though they may have heard about you.

Secondly, another way to still involve yourself with educating students but not being the teacher is to become a tutor. Advertising to become a tutor or working for tutoring companies can be very helpful to give individual attention so that the individual students can become more successful. A side benefit is that a tutor usually will not have too many discipline issues to encounter due to the fact that the student usually knows and respects the importance of this individual attention.

Another way to give personal attention to students thereby helping them is becoming a monitor or a judge for the Academic Decathlon on the county, state, and even national levels. You will encounter some of the brightest students and, quite possibly, the leaders of tomorrow. It is quite a rewarding experience to consider. If you call your county office of education or if you do a Google search, more information can be obtained.

You may want to give workshops to a school's student population, the parents and guardians, as well as the teachers. Sharing your expertise with new and veteran teachers alike can help them improve in their roles to make a positive impact on their students.

You may wish to consider presenting workshops to local, state, and national educational organizations, such as the National Educators' Association, the American Federation of Teachers, and Phi Delta Kappa. There may be an e-mentor program available through these organizations for your consideration in order to help new teachers deal with the typical problems that they experience. Thus, your guidance can be instrumental for them.

You may wish to write books to offer ideas and suggestions for prospective and current high school teachers.

If none of the above ideas sounds appealing but you still wish to do something to promote education, you may wish to consider the People to People Ambassador Programs at www.ambassadorprograms.org, which is a unique way to help other countries with their educational systems and also to meet other professionals of different fields. There is an expense on the participant's part, but if you do have the time, the inclination, and the money, this truly is a worthy way to "pay it forward," to contribute to other countries so that they may advance their education. There are also other such organizations, and they may be found by doing a Google search.

Of course, if you wish to not involve yourself with education whatsoever, you too are totally deserving of your well-earned retirement so that you can pursue whatever you wish, whether to be involved with organizations of personal interest, reading books, hobbies, learning or perfecting your skills of playing a musical instrument, and/or trips. Actually, being active in any or all of these ways is a great education as well. Then you will be developing your own lesson plan whose beneficiary will be you, your family, and your friends. Enjoy!

Teaching, the Hardest Job You Will Ever Love!: Helpful Ideas for Teachers In and Out of the Classroom has dealt with the importance of you as an individual, the improvement of your teaching ability, and your students' learning. You have probably agreed and disagreed. Please just remember that these ideas have worked, and they can help you and your students to become inspired and educated. It is essential to incorporate proven and new ideas in order to develop your own stepping stones, your unique way of reaching and teaching so your students will blossom with your guidance now and in the future.

Ultimately, teaching can be the hardest job you will ever love, and yet students can become better educated and self-accountable. Miklos Fejer, one of my former brilliant students, summarized this idea quite well: "You can make more tomorrows than a person can possibly count!" May your teaching career be filled mostly with success and with few frustrations. Congratulations for making the difference in your students' lives today and tomorrow!

~

Suggested Resources

American Federation of Teachers. http://www.aft.org.

Big Brothers Big Sisters. http://www.bbbsa.org.

Book Rags. http://www.bookrags.com.

California League of High Schools. http://www.clhs.net.

Cantinflas, Shirley MacLaine, Robert Newton, and David Niven. *Around the World in 80 Days*, DVD. Directed by Michael Anderson. Burbank, CA: Warner Home Video, 2004.

Classmates. http://www.classmates.com.

Dullea, Keir, Gary Lockwood, Daniel Richter, and William Sylvester. *2001: A Space Odyssey*, DVD. Directed by Stanley Kubrick. Burbank, CA: Warner Home Video, 2007.

Earth Google. http://www.earth.google.com.

Facebook. http://www.facebook.com.

Garcia, Andy, Rosanna de Soto, Edward James Olmos, and Lou Diamond Phillips. *Stand and Deliver*, DVD. Directed by Ramon Menendez. Burbank, CA: Warner Home Video, 2004.

Good Character. http://www.goodcharacter.com.

Griffin, John H. *Black Like Me*. Columbia: Wings Press, 2006.

Manteca High School. http://www.mantecausd.net/mhs/MantecaHighHome Page. html.

Myofascial release therapy. http://www.myofascialreleasetherapy.com.

MySpace. http://www.myspace.com.

National Education Association. http://www.nea.org.

Neuromuscular Integrative Action. http://www.nianow.com.

People to People Ambassador Programs. http://www.ambassadorprograms.org.

Phi Delta Kappa. http://www.pdkintl.org.

Skype. http://www.skype.com.

Southern Poverty Law Center. http://www.tolerance.org.

Stock, Gregory. *The Book of Questions*, New York: Workman, 1987.

———. *The Kids' Book of Questions*, New York: Workman, 2004.

Teacher Expectations and Student Achievement. http://www.streamer3.lacoe.edu/tesa.

Teacher Movie. http://www.teachermovie.com.

Toastmasters. http://www.toastmasters.org.

United States Academic Decathlon. http://www.usad.org.

You Tube. http://www.youtube.com.

~

About the Author

Steve Sonntag earned his MA in Spanish from California State University, San Francisco. He taught Spanish, German, Latin, English, and the Academic Decathlon primarily at Manteca High School in Manteca, California, for thirty-two years. He always has believed that students deserve to be heard while still maintaining realistic, high expectations for them. His flexibility helped to reach a majority of his students. He was a department chairperson and the high school's accreditation chairperson. He has evaluated three high schools. He was a mentor teacher and the high school teacher of the year in the Manteca Unified School District. He taught Spanish at San Joaquin Delta College in Stockton, California, for sixteen years. He also has taught medical Spanish for Chapman University and for California State University, Stanislaus in Stockton, California, for a total of three semesters.